WITHDRAWAL

Standards Deviation

Standards Deviation

HOW SCHOOLS MISUNDERSTAND EDUCATION POLICY

James P. Spillane

Harvard University Press
Cambridge, Massachusetts
London, England
2004

LIBRARY OF CONGRESS CATALOGING-IN-PUBLICATION DATA

Spillane, James P.
  Standards deviation : how schools misunderstand education policy / James P. Spillane.
    p.   cm.
  Includes bibliographical references and index.
  ISBN 0-674-01323-9 (cloth : alk. paper)
    1. Education and state–United States.   2. Education–Standards–United States.
    I. Title.
  LC89.S54   2004
379.73–dc22   2003067510

March 31, 2004

Contents

Acknowledgments

This book has benefited greatly from the generosity of many. I am especially thankful to the more than 450 teachers, school administrators, district office officials, and state policymakers in Michigan who gave generously of their time. The work also benefited from a wonderful research team—Angie Eshelman, S. G. Grant, Nancy Jennings, Loyiso Jita, Chris Lubienski, Chris Reimann, Charles Thompson, Kyle Ward, and John Zeuli. I am especially grateful to Charles Thompson for collaborating with me on the design and execution of the research. A number of consultants to the project enriched the work, especially Deborah Ball, David Cohen, Peg Goertz, Pam Jakwerth, Aaron Pallas, and Bill Schmidt. The work also improved as a result of input by the Michigan Statewide Systemic Initiative Steering Committee.

The book would not have been possible without the National Science Foundation, which provided the financial resources for the research (Grant No. OSR-9250061). In addition, the support of Northwestern University's Institute for Policy Research (IPR) and School of Education and Social Policy was critical during the writing phase of the book. I thank both Dean Penelope Peterson and IPR Director Fay Cook for their very generous support. Further, I owe a big thanks to my colleagues in the School of Education and Social Policy and Institute for Policy Research for creating a rich environment for learning and dialogue. I am very appreciative of the Consortium for Policy Research in Education (CPRE), especially Susan Fuhrman, for its support throughout this endeavor.

Earlier versions of Chapters 5 and 7 were published, respectively, as J. Spillane and C. Thompson, "Reconstructing Conceptions of Local Capacity: The Local Education Agency's Capacity for Ambitious Instructional Reform," vol. 19, no. 2 (1997): 185–203, and J. Spillane and J. Zeuli, "Reform and Mathematics Teaching: Exploring Patterns of Practice in the Context of National and State Reforms," vol. 21, no. 1 (1999): 1–27, both from *Educational Evaluation and Policy Analysis,* © American Educational Research Association. Reprinted with the permission of the publisher. My coauthors on these articles deserve special thanks.

Over the years I have been blessed by a wealth of colleagues who have given me generously of their time and insights. While I cannot possibly mention everyone by name, the book has benefited tremendously from the comments of Deborah Ball, Allan Collins, Corey Drake, Danny Edelson, Dick Elmore, Susan Fuhrman, Karen Fuson, Louis Gomez, Richard Halverson, Fred Hess, Heather Hill, Barton Hirch, Maggie Lampert, Dan Lewis, Marjorie Orellano, Andrew Ortony, Penelope Peterson, Jeremy Price, Brian Reiser, Lauren Resnick, Jennifer Romich, Bruce Sherin, Mirian Sherin, Gary Sykes, Charles Thompson, Beth van Es, Suzanne Wilson, and John Zeuli. Their support and insights helped improve the work. I also owe a very special thanks to my mentor, David Cohen. For more than a decade he has given generously of his time, council, and friendship, and this book is far better as a result. I could not have asked for a better teacher.

Graduate and undergraduate students at Northwestern have been an invaluable resource in this process. I especially thank the undergraduate students Erica Brasier, Brandon Miller, and Amy Ottesen for their help with data analysis. I thank Julie Carlson, Marsha Coffey, as well as Mary Lou Manning, for their help with editing, tables, and references. My editor, Elizabeth Knoll, deserves a special note of appreciation for her critique and encouragement throughout the process.

My immediate and extended family have always provided unwavering support, even from a distance. I am very grateful. And I have been blessed with a network of friends in Chicago and beyond whose friendship over the years has made this book possible. I thank Chelsea for her unconditional companionship throughout.

Finally, I am indebted to my partner and best friend, Richard Czuba, to whom I owe thanks for over a decade of unwavering love and support. He has endured the late nights, moods, doubts, and worries that come with such a project. Moreover, his very frank appraisal of an earlier draft inspired me to rewrite. Together with Elizabeth Knoll, he suggested the telephone-game metaphor and persuaded me to use it in the book. Without his friendship, this project would never have come to fruition.

Of course, I alone am responsible for the views expressed or the errors made in the pages that follow.

Standards Deviation

CHAPTER 1

Making Education Policy Here, There, and Everywhere

Aᴅᴍɪɴɪsᴛʀᴀᴛᴏʀs ᴀɴᴅ ᴛᴇᴀᴄʜᴇʀs in Lakeside school district,* far from the hubbub of state policymaking, became increasingly busy with education policy during the 1990s. Tucked away on the southern shore of Lake Superior in northern Michigan, Lakeside enrolls fewer than a thousand students and has a district office made up of a superintendent, assistant superintendent, and secretary. In Lakeside, Ann Smith, a full-time teacher, was the district's chief instructional policymaker for science during the 1990s. With a committee of teacher volunteers, Smith, a twenty-year veteran of Lakeside's middle school, spearheaded the district's efforts to develop policies for K–12 science education. These policies were designed to fundamentally revise what science content was to be taught, when and how it was to be taught, and which classroom materials were to be used. Smith's soft-spoken manner belies her self-described risk-taking, take-charge, "type A" personal-

---

* All names used in this book are pseudonyms.

ity. She wrote a grant and was awarded $150,000 by a private foundation to fund rewriting the district's science policy and to develop professional development and materials to support its implementation. To accomplish this, Smith said that they used SEMS Plus, Michigan Goals and Objectives, California Frameworks, as well as other reform documents to develop a mission statement and to articulate curriculum outcomes.

Lakeside's policymaking initiatives were in good company. State policymakers were also busy developing state learning standards for science education and revising the state's student assessment system. At the national level, school reformers and professional associations were also developing learning standards for K–12 science education. Up and down the education system, instructional policymaking was a growth industry.

As Ann Smith saw it, Lakeside's policymaking initiatives were informed by state and national policymaking efforts. But Smith and her colleagues also turned to other sources to develop their district's science policy, including state policies from California and Wisconsin, policies from other school districts, Project 2061 —an initiative by the National Academy of Sciences to improve K–12 education—and science education experts at a local university. "When we wrote it," she explained with respect to Lakeside's policy for science education, "we realized that we were drawing from some of the big sources—Project 2061 and other major sources—that were out there." Michigan's state-level policy about science education "added impetus" to Lakeside's policymaking initiatives, enabling local policymakers to put pressure on those teachers who thought that school-district reform efforts would "blow over."

Smith's goals for K–12 science education in Lakeview were, as she put it, "pretty lofty," easily as ambitious as those pressed by state and national policymakers. She pushed for "overwhelming change," not only in the content of the science curriculum, but also in the way in which teachers taught that content. She wanted

K–12 students to be exposed to core scientific concepts and to understand relationships among these concepts. She wanted students to learn how to use scientific theories and concepts to set up, carry out, and critique their own and others' scientific investigations. These were radical ideas when contrasted with science instruction in most classrooms, where learning focused on memorizing isolated bits of knowledge and where doing science involved following recipes for "cookbook" experiments. These directions are all the more remarkable considering that Ann Smith was not a science major and for the first half of her career in the classroom was, in her own words, "a textbook science teacher" who did "the traditional biology labs of dissection and so forth."

All was not smooth sailing for Smith and her fellow local policymakers. Lakeside's science policy met with resistance from elementary schoolteachers. Smith found herself, as she put it, "out front and taking the shots" as teachers voiced their objections.

Making Education Policy in the 1990s

From a national perspective, Lakeside's education policymaking efforts were not unusual. Since the 1980s, U.S. public policymakers have taken up ever more complex social problems, using policy in an attempt to leverage change in local behavior and alleviate a variety of social ills. Perhaps nowhere have these ambitions been more evident than in education; federal, state, and local government policymakers have attempted wide-ranging changes in K–12 schools and classrooms in an effort to improve learning opportunities for all American children. This reform deluge has included proposals for school-based management and restructuring, parental choice, state standards and policy alignment, whole school reform, and charter schools.

Standards-based reform has gained popularity with policymakers and school reformers in the last couple of decades. The "standards movement," as it is commonly known, gained momentum in the 1980s—garnering attention from policymakers at all levels of the education system. Professional associations, federal policymakers, and state governments, many of which had taken a "hands-off" approach on instructional matters, pressed standards-based reform. They developed curricular frameworks that defined challenging learning standards and aligned policies with these standards. Many local school districts, like Lakeside, also took to these ideas about improving education. Further, widely touted forecasts in the 1990s of the demise of the standards movement were premature; standards occupy a central plank in President Bush's education agenda. Indeed, the movement's resilience makes it something of an oddity in education, where fads are customary.

Regardless of its resilience, standards-based reform initiatives face a familiar policy challenge—successful local implementation. This book explores this subject by examining the role of local school districts, like Lakeside, in the implementation of state and national standards. Occupying an intermediary position between the statehouse and the schoolhouse, the school district has the potential to influence the implementation of state and national policies. Contrary to predictions of their demise, the school district remains a central governing entity in American education.

Despite all this, the school district has received sparse attention in policymakers' and researchers' discussions about reforming schools. State government, schools, and classrooms have figured prominently in these discussions and research on standards-based reform, but the local school district has fallen through the cracks. In an effort to address this void, I focus on the local school district and its role in the implementation of state and national standards. I investigate whether and how school districts carry out the ideas about instruction pressed by standards and look at the consequences of what districts do and do not do in this regard. Further, I consider how interactions among national, state, and district policies are played out in schools and classrooms.

The issue is complex in part because, as the Lakeside example illuminates, Smith and her colleagues were making policy about science education; they were not simply carrying out the proposals of state policymakers. While state policies figured in Lakeside's policymaking about science education, they were but one source of ideas, and not even the most important one. Viewing the school district as a policymaking agency is important.

Moving beyond a descriptive account of how districts implement higher-level policies, I develop a theoretical and empirical basis for a cognitive perspective on state and local government relations on matters of instruction. Using one state's effort to develop and implement mathematics and science standards, I examine what happens as these standards percolate through the system between the statehouse and the schoolhouse. As state policymakers' appetite for instructional policymaking increases, what role does the school district play? Exploring state and national standards from the perspective of district policymakers and teachers, I consider the interplay of state and school-district policymaking and explore how this interactive policymaking plays out in classrooms.

Framing Intergovernmental Relations

The local official has a great deal of discretion vis-à-vis federal and state policies (Lipsky, 1980). Teachers, district and school administrators, and other locals often fail to notice, intentionally ignore, or selectively attend to policies, especially those that are inconsistent with their own agendas.

Unpacking local discretion as currently understood in policy analysis, I develop a cognitive model that illuminates the interplay between the government policies that attempt to guide local action and the way in which local officials construct that action.

By concentrating on how local actors understand their behavior as a result of federal and state policy initiatives, I explore an aspect of the implementation process that has remained largely implicit in previous work.

Conventional Accounts

Many conventional models are premised on principal-agent and rational choice theories in which utility maximization governs decision making. Rational choice theory assumes that the act of choosing is at the center of an individual's life, that individual preferences are neither vague nor contradictory, and that all choices are reduced to personal interest or to utility maximization (Moessinger, 2000). In conventional accounts, policies fail to get implemented because the policy is muddled or weak, or because it does not fit with the interests of utility-maximizing local officials. Autonomous local officials are thought to intentionally close their eyes to or selectively attend to policies that are inconsistent with their interests and agendas (Firestone, 1989).

Conventional accounts assume that local officials are choosing between following policymakers' directions or ignoring them; they assume that locals get the intended policy message. That assumption is problematic because in order to choose, local actors must figure out what the policy means. To decide whether to ignore, alter, or adopt policymakers' recommendations, local officials must construct an understanding of the policy message. When conventional accounts consider local interpretations of policy, local actors are depicted, implicitly or explicitly, as willfully interpreting policy to make it fit their own agendas—whereas in fact they may just misunderstand what policymakers are asking them to do.

Some scholars have critiqued the inattention to the social contexts in which individuals choose and the overemphasis on the actions of self-interested individuals in the achievement of optimum outcomes. Another problem with conventional models concerns their portrayal of local officials as saboteurs working to circumvent policies that do not advance their self-interests. Recent research suggests that bureaucrats tend to be hardworking; they do not typically work to undermine policy directives from above (Brehm and Gates, 1997). In addition, recent implementation studies suggest that teachers and administrators frequently not only heed higher-level policies but also work diligently to implement these policies (EEPA, 1990; Firestone, Fitz, and Broadfoot, 1999). Yet the same studies offer ample evidence of limited local implementation of state policies, suggesting that local officials' resistance does not account for implementation failure.

A Cognitive Account

Implementation scholars working in the cognitive tradition argue that the ideas that local officials come to understand from policy are an integral, though largely unexplored, component of the implementation process (Cohen and Weiss, 1993; Hill, 1999; Lin, 2000; Yanow, 1996). If local officials respond to higher-level policy, they respond to the ideas about local behavior that they construct from policy. This sense-making process is fraught with opportunities for understandings to develop that do not reflect those intended by policymakers.

This book foregrounds how district policymakers and teachers make sense of standards and in the process select the cues and signals that they interpret (Weick, 1995). Inundated with signals from their environment, people notice some and ignore most others, as they use the lenses they have developed through experience to filter their awareness. Indeed, part of sense-making involves categorizing signals into some sort of framework (Starbuck and Milliken, 1988). Having noticed and categorized signals, individuals interpret them. Coming to know, then, involves the reconstruction of existing knowledge rather than the passive absorption of knowledge from signals (Anderson and Smith, 1987; Confrey, 1990).

From a cognitive perspective, policy signals do not present solutions as givens that local officials choose to ignore or implement. Instead, local officials must construct what the proposal is and then figure out what it entails for their current behavior. Cognition is complex, and misunderstandings are commonplace. Hence, local officials' failure to do what policymakers ask can result from honest misunderstandings rather than willful attempts to adapt policy to suit their own ends.

As policy moves from the capitol to the classroom, school districts work to figure out what the policy means for their work. School-district officials make sense of the policy and pass their understandings on to school leaders and teachers. Private consultants, professional development providers, professional associations, and others outside the formal school system develop their own understandings of the policy, which they pass along to administrators and teachers through workshops, consultations, and other means. Of course, school leaders and teachers may already have worked out an understanding of the "new" policy.

Policy implementation is like the telephone game: the player at the start of the line tells a story to the next person in line who then relays the story to the third person in line, and so on. Of course, by the time the story is retold by the final player to everyone it is very different from the original story. The story is morphed as it moves from player to player—characters change, protagonists become antagonists, new plots emerge. This happens not because the players are intentionally trying to change the story; it happens because that is the nature of human sense-making.

Standards-Based Reform: Origins, Design, and Goals

From a historical perspective, standards represent substantial shifts in education policymaking. One shift concerns the more active engagement of government, especially state government, in instructional policymaking. Another shift concerns the ambi-

tiousness of the changes that government has been seeking—
changes that move beyond specifying minimum learning compe-
tencies and pressing for more intellectually rigorous instruction
and academically challenging learning outcomes.

Origins and Design

For more than a decade now, standards-based reform has become
something of a mantra among state and national policymakers.
Critiquing the incoherence of most states' instructional policies
as well as policymakers' propensity for piecemeal approaches to
reform, advocates of standards argue for a systemwide or systemic
approach to school improvement. These school reformers suggest
that the reform initiatives of the 1970s and early 1980s, which
stressed top-down mandates such as minimum competency testing, did not produce substantial improvement in instruction but
rather reinforced the school system's emphasis on basic skills
(Smith and O'Day, 1991). The standards movement, with its
stress on systemic initiatives, was designed to address these short-
comings.

State and federal policymakers have never before taken such a
keen interest in classroom instruction, mobilizing public policy
to transform instruction in fundamental ways. While school reformers such as John Dewey and the Progressives attempted to
fundamentally transform the classroom experience of America's
children, their attempts were mostly orchestrated from outside
government rather than by government. During the 1950s there
were considerable efforts at the national level, especially by the
National Science Foundation (NSF), to fundamentally improve
the quality of science and mathematics education. But these efforts involved government only indirectly, for example, by means
of NSF's financial support for curriculum development. The standards movement has involved a much more active role for state
government and federal agencies in matters of classroom instruction.

Standards define what students should know and be able to do in core subjects at critical points in their formal schooling. Designs for standards-based reform involve four core elements:

development of curricular frameworks,
alignment of state policies,
teacher professional development, and
development of accountability mechanisms.

First, the point of departure for standards-based reform is the establishment of state curricular frameworks that attempt to define in a clear and measurable way what all students should know. A second element involves the alignment of other state instructional policies including student assessment, curricular materials, professional development, teacher education, and accountability for following these frameworks. A third element involves professional development in order to reeducate teachers to teach to the standards. The fourth element concerns the development and deployment of mechanisms that hold schools accountable for students' achievement (see McLaughlin and Shepard, 1995; Smith and O'Day, 1991).

Policymakers across the system, especially state policymakers, have welcomed these ideas for improving K–12 education. Indicators of the movement's progress are impressive. The annual review of standards from 1995 to 1999 by the American Federation of Teachers (AFT) demonstrates that during this period these ideas about improving America's schools have garnered support from more and more states. For example, the AFT review in 1999 concluded that the number of states that had standards that met the AFT's criteria increased from 13 in 1995 to 22 in 1999, and the number of states that had or were planning assessments jumped from 33 to 49 in the same time period. Similarly, while only three states had promotion policies based on the achievement of their standards in 1996, thirteen states had such policies by 1999.

Lofty Ambitions

The standards movement set its aims high, calling for more intellectually demanding content and pedagogy for all American children. It challenged deeply rooted beliefs about who could do intellectually demanding work. The standards movement also challenged popular conceptions of what it means to teach, learn, and know school subjects. Standards-based reform sought tremendous changes in classroom instruction, pressing teachers to engage their students with more intellectually demanding academic content. Being able to recite multiplication tables or regurgitate on demand the formula for finding the volume of a sphere, while necessary, was no longer deemed sufficient for America's children. Children were also to learn, beginning in elementary school, about key mathematical and scientific concepts. They were to develop an appreciation for doing mathematics that involved more than memorizing and computing—it was to involve problem solving and justifying one's mathematical procedures and solutions. America's school reformers had developed a taste for more intellectually challenging academic work. Satisfying this appetite would necessitate tremendous change in the instructional practices prevalent in most K–12 classrooms.

Such change would not be easy. Decades of research suggested that classroom practice was resilient to policy and other reform initiatives (Cuban, 1993; Fullan, 1991; Meyer and Rowan, 1978; Tyack and Tobin, 1994). Prior policies that sought modest changes compared with the standards often failed to get beyond the classroom door. If compliance is the goal of the policy implementation processes, then changing local behavior through public policy is tricky because local officials have considerable discretion.

Standards-based reform, then, posed a familiar subject for policy scholars—local implementation. If previous scholarship was roughly right, we would expect that the standards movement would have been scuttled to the school reform scrap heap. More-over, at best we would expect standards to have only modest and fleeting effects on teachers' instructional practices. But almost twenty years in, standards-based reform has many disciples, especially among state and federal policymakers. Moreover, recent studies suggest that these initiatives have influenced classroom instruction, albeit not uniformly (EEPA, 1990; Firestone, Fitz, and Broadfoot, 1999).

Standards-Based Reform and Intergovernmental Relations

Reinventing Instructional Governance

The standards movement also involved an effort to reinvent arrangements for governing instruction. Traditionally, responsibility for instructional governance has been fragmented and localized in the United States; schools and school districts played leading roles while state and federal agencies played supporting roles. The standards movement envisioned a more active role for state governments. It involved state government exercising its legal and political authority over education and deploying a variety of policy instruments to get local educators to heed its guidance on matters of instruction. While standards were typically determined at the state or national level, the responsibility for deciding how to achieve these goals (for example, the selection of curricular materials) was left to schools (O'Day and Smith, 1993). Reformers appeared intent on putting individual schools in more direct contact with state guidance for instruction. Under these arrangements, state government and the local school administrators were the pivotal instructional decision-making entities, with the local school district being assigned a supporting role.

The local school district did not figure prominently in standards-based reform prototypes or policies. As conceived by its designers and reflected in state policy initiatives, the standards movement was relatively quiet on the local school district's role. Some commentators viewed the school district as an impediment to change; they cautioned school districts against "usurping" school and state roles and encouraged them to support the efforts of individual schools to meet the standards (Smith and O'Day, 1991). Key elements of standards-based reform initiatives in many states bypassed the school district altogether, targeting the school head-on.

Such modest attention to school districts was not new; state governments and schools have featured more prominently in school reform proposals for a few decades. Still, history suggests that district office administrators are crucial in mobilizing local support for the successful implementation of state and federal policy (Berman and McLaughlin, 1977). The school district's policies on professional development, curriculum, teacher supervision, and so forth can amplify, "drown out," or minimize the salience of state-initiated reforms for teachers (Spillane, 1996). Further, school districts are the chief decision makers about teachers' professional development, which is crucial if teachers are to acquire the skills and knowledge that are typically necessary to successfully implement state and federal policies (Little, 1989). Moreover, in most states the school district continued to be an important source of revenue generation through local taxation. Finally, most state departments of education lacked the resources necessary to support and monitor the implementation of their policies. With limited resources, state departments of education depended on the local school district to follow through on the implementation of their standards.

Thus the limited attention to the school district in standards-based reform initiatives was somewhat puzzling. What role was the local school district to take on matters of instructional governance as states developed standards-based reform initiatives? A historical perspective provides us with a foundation from which to consider the response of the local school district to state government efforts to exercise more influence over classroom instruction.

Intergovernmental Relations: A Retrospective

From a historical perspective, state standards initiatives represented a considerable accomplishment for states, especially states with histories of deference to local control. The school district is the basic administrative unit of school governance in the United States, a position it has held for almost a century. While most states began to play a much more active role in instructional policymaking, beginning in the 1970s and continuing into the 1990s with standards-based reform, and although school districts were constitutionally creatures of the state by virtue of political tradition, they had a great deal of authority that was unlikely to dissipate regardless of standards-based reform initiatives.

Matters of state and local relations on instructional matters in most American states are far from settled. Tensions and interdependencies among levels of government, and among different centers of authority within each level, are uniquely American, products of a federalist system of government. Whereas public schooling in most developed nations is a creation of the nation-state, constructed from the center based on the authority, funds, and governing structures of national governments or colonial powers (Ramirez and Boli, 1987), circumstances are entirely different in the United States, where schooling is a creation of local communities. As the public education enterprise grew in the United States, therefore, much of the political and administrative terrain of schooling remained ill-defined, waiting to be charted and filled in over time. Successive waves of school reform, including the standards movement, have contributed to charting some of this vast administrative and political territory, but it is still very much a work in progress, especially when contrasted with national education systems in some other countries.

The U.S. Constitution makes no provision for education. Rather, state governments are given responsibility for such matters under the Tenth Amendment. Beginning in the 1860s, state governments began to enact education legislation more vigorously, passing compulsory school-attendance laws and laying out minimum standards for school buildings, equipment, and teacher qualifications (Wirt and Kirst, 1997). Lacking resources, staff, and funding, however, states had no way of enforcing these laws.

Although the local school district emerged as a legal unit of school government as early as 1789 in Massachusetts, it was a century later before most states established school districts as legal entities (Butts and Cremin, 1953; Dexter, 1922). While having a superintendent of schools became commonplace in urban school systems in the second half of the nineteenth century, the superintendents' influence was curtailed because they had few resources and were at the mercy of lay boards who decided most issues pertaining to schools (Tyack and Hansot, 1982). Circumstances changed some in the early part of the twentieth century with the emergence of the Progressive movement, especially in larger cities. Frederick Taylor's efficiency management scheme, based on hierarchical control of work by breaking tasks into their constituent parts and allocating responsibility for these subtasks to different positions in the hierarchy, became the dominant organizing scheme for business in the early part of the century. Advanced through the National Education Association (NEA) and through university programs, these ideas were adopted and adapted by urban school administrators eager to advance their position and legitimacy.

Still, large city school systems were the exception rather than the rule, and in most local school systems the district office did not develop the administrative infrastructure to carry out the work of guiding instruction. A scarcity of funding, accentuated by the onslaught of the Depression and expanding student enrollments, curtailed district office efforts to take an active role in governing instruction. Thus, a de facto compromise developed during the first half of the twentieth century: all authority at the center, but with individual schools and classrooms bearing huge operating responsibility. In most places, schools continued to make instructional policy themselves; they selected texts and materials and decided on curriculum content, with most district offices playing a modest role at best.

Circumstances changed in the 1960s as government agencies began to define their roles in school governance. The federal government took a more active role in public education, albeit indirectly, beginning with the National Defense Education Act in the late 1950s. Federal funding of education continued to expand during the 1960s, most notably with the Elementary and Secondary Education Act (ESEA) passed by Congress in 1965. Through an array of different programs, these legislative initiatives contributed large amounts of money to America's schools. Most important, these federal dollars were dispersed through state and local government agencies. Hence, federal programs nurtured the capacity of state and local government agencies to engage in instructional governance by enabling them to hire additional personnel. Further, these federal programs defined new tasks and responsibilities for state and local government agencies. For example, the Title 1 program of ESEA made the state department of education the principal oversight agency for ESEA's local implementation, while the local school district became the chief administrative agency for the program. The bulk of federal Title 1 funds was routed through the school district to local schools. In these ways, federal programs defined new roles and responsibilities for state and local government agencies and helped legitimate their involvement in matters of school governance.

Federal funding for education increased through numerous unrelated programs, what John Meyer and Richard Scott (1983) called "fragmented centralization." These distinct programs generated new resources and also defined new responsibilities for state governments and local school districts. State agencies and district offices managed the administrative load that fragmented federal programs created for them by expanding their administrative operations into complex segmented organizational arrangements that reflected the distinct as well as often unrelated federal programs (Cohen, 1982; Meyer, Scott, and Strang, 1987; Rowan, 1982). For example, state departments of education and school districts established Title 1 units and positions to administer the federal Title 1 program established by the ESEA of 1965. Increased state policymaking had a similar effect at the school-district level (Cohen, 1982; Rowan, 1982).

Fueled by national reports and public concern about basic skills, state governments, even in states where local control had well-established roots, began to assert their constitutional authority in the 1970s, establishing core curricula and statewide assessment programs. But one should not confuse constitutional authority with political authority: much of the state legislation that expanded the state's role in instructional governance did little to curtail or dampen the school district's role in such matters. The same public concerns that pressed states into action also prompted school districts to attend more to instructional issues. Further, even though state governments became more active in these matters by hiring more staff and spending more money to develop and administer mechanisms for governing instruction (for example, student assessment instruments), their zeal for such work far outpaced their capacity for it. Most state departments of education had only a handful of consultants in key subject areas such as language arts, mathematics, and science to provide technical assistance to the thousands of teachers who taught these subjects in their state. Hence, states relied on school districts to help implement their instructional policies.

Standards-Based Reform: What Role for the School District?
Some observers have argued that as federal and state governments expand their policymaking activity, local government decision-making contracts (Wise, 1979). Others saw the expanding state

role in education as forecasting the downfall of the local school district (Cantor, 1981).

Other analysts have questioned the conventional wisdom that increased state and federal policy activity lessens the school districts' decision-making activity, suggesting that centralization of instructional governance and policymaking at the state or federal level does not result in shrinking the instructional policymaking activities of the school district (Cohen 1982; Fuhrman and Elmore, 1990). The historical evidence reviewed earlier favors this perspective, suggesting that educational policymaking is not a zero-sum game: Federal, state, and local government policymaking have expanded in tandem, often encouraged and informed by similar sources (for example, public opinion or national reports). Following no great design or central plan, efforts to govern at different levels of the system frequently paralleled each other. Policy initiatives at higher levels of the system did little to dampen the enthusiasm of lower levels of the system for making policy. Federal education policy initiatives contributed to the expansion of state instructional policymaking, just as federal and state initiatives contributed to policymaking in the local school district.

If history is a reasonably reliable guide, then, we can expect that state standards initiatives are unlikely to curtail instructional policymaking in local school districts. Indeed, we might expect that state standards would contribute to instructional policymaking in the school district. The situation in Lakeside public schools suggests as much. The fact that state policymakers in Michigan developed policies about science education did nothing to dampen that school district's policymaking efforts. If anything, state standards had the opposite effect, adding momentum to local instructional policymaking efforts in Lakeside.

These circumstances complicate the implementation of standards and efforts to study this process. While the core concern remains whether and how state and national policymakers can get local officials to practice in new ways, some local actors in this instance are policymakers in their own right. Casting school districts as implementing agencies, policy analysts focus their work on the extent to which local agencies such as school districts "put into practice" the policy proposals of higher-level agencies. But school districts have made and are likely to continue to make instructional policy. Ann Smith and her colleagues in Lakeside were involved in making policy about science education, and while state standards were featured in this work, the implementation of these standards was not what defined it. Hence, in my investigation of the local implementation of standards-based reform, I acknowledged the school district as a policymaking entity rather than casting it exclusively or chiefly as a policy implementing entity and considered the following questions: As state governments and national agencies develop standards to guide instruction, what role does the school district play? How does the school district respond to state and national standards? How is the school district's role in instructional decision making changed as state policymakers develop clearer and more authoritative guidance on matters of classroom instruction? And what influence, if any, do the school district's initiatives on matters of instruction have on the implementation of state and national standards at the classroom level?

Preview

Through a case study of Michigan's standards-based reform initiatives, I explore the cognitive dimensions of intergovernmental relations in the following chapters. Chapter 2 investigates Michigan's efforts to develop mathematics and science standards and explores both the content and context of state standards. Chapters 3 through 5 investigate the response of the local school district to standards from the perspective of policymakers in nine diverse Michigan school districts. District policymakers included district office and school administrators, curriculum specialists, and classroom teachers who, by virtue of formal position or informal role, craft school-district policies about instruction. Chapter 3 considers how state standards played out in the school districts' instructional policymaking, documenting uneven support for standards among districts. Contrasting districts that provided high support for standards with those districts that did not, in Chapter 4 I develop a cognitive explanation to account for this variation. Chapter 5 examines the school district's capacity for making sense from and about the standards.

Chapters 6 and 7 consider standards from the perspective of classroom teachers. Chapter 6 investigates what teachers in the nine school districts made of standards and their school districts' policies about mathematics and science. Taking a closer look at teachers' practice, in Chapter 7 I document how the ideas promoted by standards progressed unevenly between classrooms. In Chapter 8 I consider what a cognitive model of implementation entails for policy analysis, policy research, and policy design.

A Word on Methods

I investigated policy implementation as distinct from "policy outcomes." Some policy analysts focus on policy outcomes, investigating whether or not a policy generated the anticipated or intended effects on the target group. With respect to the mathematics and science standards, attention to policy outcomes might focus on whether and the extent to which Michigan schoolchildren's mathematics and science achievement improved as a result of the standards. Measuring outcomes is difficult, especially absent randomization, which is often complicated in the education policy arena. If, for example, Michigan schoolteachers did what the mathematics standards asked of them and we found that the mathematics achievement of Michigan children increased substantially over a decade or so, then we might be able to say something about the positive outcomes of the mathematics standards. Still, absent some firm evidence about the extent to which Michigan teachers had implemented the mathematics standards, it would be difficult to draw conclusions about the relationship between the standards and student achievement. Policy analysts often jump to the question of effects, skipping or glossing over whether the policy was implemented as designed. Measuring policy outcomes absent attention to the extent to which the policy was implemented is problematic because it is difficult to gauge the effects of a policy that was not fully implemented (Lin, 2000).

To study the policy implementation process, I examined Michigan's state standards-based initiatives around mathematics and science education in the 1990s and then investigated how these initiatives played out in a diverse sample of Michigan school districts and classrooms. Because my primary objective was to build a theory about the implementation process, the most sensible research strategy involved a case study approach in a single state and in strategically sampled school districts (to maximize variability) within that state.

This book uses empirical data from a four-year study of relations between state and national standards, local school-district policymaking, and classroom practice undertaken in Michigan between 1992 and 1996. I used mixed methods, including semistructured interviews, questionnaires, and observations. Concentrating on mathematics and science education, the first phase of the study examined the state policy system using in-depth interviews with state policymakers and a review of policy documents. In the second phase, a multisite case study was used to collect and analyze data about the school district's role with respect to state and national standards. The third and final phase of the study explored the effects of national, state, and district mathematics and science policies in classrooms in the nine school districts. Methodological issues are addressed in detail in the Appendix.

Excerpts from interviews and questionnaires have been lightly edited to improve their readability.

CHAPTER 2

Doing Standards: Content and Context

THE STANDARDS-BASED REFORM MOVEMENT gathered momentum in the late 1980s as state policymakers looked to these ideas for fixing America's schools. States developed their own takes on standards-based reform, adapting the prototype to their unique political, historical, and institutional contexts. As a result, approaches to standards-based reform varied from one state to the next. Moreover, state policymakers' fondness for novelty contributed to unsettled state policy environments where change rather than stability was the norm. Hence the form, and sometimes the content, of standards-based reform efforts shifted over time with changes in state political and policy circumstances.

Standards-based reform received considerable attention from school reformers and policymakers in Michigan, a state with a tradition of local control on matters of education. While reform efforts began with reading, attention to mathematics and science followed soon. By the mid- to late 1980s, two loose coalitions of state education officials, academics, and school professionals were revising state policies to emphasize ideas about mathematics and science education that contrasted sharply with past state policies. These reformers had grand ambitions for what and how Michigan's youth should learn about mathematics and science in school. Their ambitions overlapped with substantial shifts in state education policy, as state government increasingly exercised its constitutional authority on educational matters.

The Content of State Standards

Despite a history of deference to local control, state policymakers in Michigan have taken a keener interest in instructional issues since the 1970s. The state specified "Essential Goals and Objectives" for reading, mathematics, and science and used the statewide Michigan Educational Assessment Program (MEAP) to measure student achievement at intermittent grades. State policymakers expanded the MEAP to include science and social studies during the 1980s and 1990s.

State reformers' appetite for instructional policymaking not only increased but also changed in the mid- to late 1980s, as state education officials, together with academics and school professionals, acquired a taste for more intellectually rigorous education. Encouraged and informed by national standards, they worked to shift the emphasis of the state's Essential Goals and Objectives from an exclusive focus on minimum skills to a focus that included intellectually challenging academic content. Michigan's science and mathematics policymakers were ambitious; they sought nothing less than a major shift in the K–12 science and mathematics curriculum. As one of the state's science coordinators put it, "I think we've sent a very clear message to the state that we mean for things to be quite different in science and that we are closely aligned with the national direction."

New Directions in Mathematics Education

Ambitions often outstrip capacity. With a single mathematics coordinator and two science coordinators, the Michigan Department of Education (MDE) was ill-equipped to revise the state's Essential Goals and Objectives for mathematics and science, let alone support their local implementation. Relying a great deal on university academics, local educators, and professional associations—the Michigan Council of Teachers of Mathematics (MCTM) and Michigan Science Teachers Association (MSTA)—the MDE revised the state's Essential Goals and Objectives. One of the MDE's science coordinators explained: "We always draw from MSTA when we are putting together any major effort in the state, and MSTA is more than willing and always supportive of helping us . . . MSTA has been an active force in supporting the direction of science education." An alliance of state officials, members of professional associations, and local administrators and teachers put together the state's new direction in science and mathematics education and revised state policies to reflect this direction.

Drawing on efforts by the National Council of Teachers of Mathematics (NCTM) to articulate national standards for mathematics education, the MDE revised its goals and objectives for mathematics education. The revised state standards detailed student learning outcomes for different mathematics topics including algebra, statistics and probability, and fractions, for grades K–3, 4–6, and 7–9. But more fundamental shifts in content coverage were also pressed: NCTM urged substantial shifts in both mathematics content and pedagogy. With respect to mathematics content, NCTM pushed for a more balanced K–12 curriculum that paid attention to both procedural and principled mathematical knowledge. Reformers wanted students to learn about mathematical concepts and to appreciate connections between these concepts and procedural mathematical knowledge. Getting teachers to pay more attention to principled mathematical knowledge was at the core of the state's efforts. As the MDE's mathematics consultant explained: "I think the goals were proceeded by the NCTM goals. I think our goal in the past was to develop proficiency with [mathematical] procedures. That as a goal has to change so that kids can value mathematics . . . We brought out our objectives and the focus was to limit the extent to which we want students [engaged] with procedural work." Pressing changes in what counted as mathematical knowledge, the state standards sought changes that went beyond the coverage and sequencing of mathematics topics. This represented a substantial shift for the state's existing policies, which emphasized procedural mathematical knowledge.

But NCTM and Michigan's mathematics reformers sought more. National and state standards proposed that students' experiences with mathematics should involve more than the memorization and application of mathematical procedures and rules. Under four broad themes—mathematics as problem solving, mathematics as communication, mathematics as reasoning, and mathematical connections—NCTM (1989, 1991) argued for changes in how America's children did mathematics in school. According to NCTM, problem solving should be threaded through the entire mathematics program, providing a context for learning both principled and procedural knowledge. Mathematics as communication, as described by NCTM, should permeate the curriculum because students need to appreciate mathematics as a way of talking about and representing mathematical ideas in different ways (for example, symbolic, verbal, pictorial, concrete). With respect to mathematics as reasoning, NCTM argued that students should have opportunities to make conjectures, build arguments in support of their mathematical thinking, and justify their solutions and reasoning. NCTM also argued that students should learn to make connections between mathematics and their own daily lives as well as connections among mathematical concepts and concepts in other subjects. Informed by recent developments on how students learn and the sort of teaching necessary to support that learning, state standards also sought changes in mathematics pedagogy. The state's mathematics coordinator explained, "The shift that we were going through at that time was a shift away from a behaviorist perspective to what I think I would consider now a constructivist perspective."

The MDE's standards for mathematics education were fairly compatible with national standards (Goertz, Floden, and O'Day, 1995). Still, while the state standards promoted fundamental changes in mathematics content, these ideas were not developed in depth or detail. Indeed, the state's mathematics standards were not nearly as well elaborated as the state's science standards. As we will see in the next section, by detailing key content and pedagogical issues concerning particular objectives, the science standards provided more elaboration than did the mathematics standards with respect to pedagogical and the more substantive content shifts.

New Ambitions for Science Education

Drawing heavily on *Science for All Americans* (American Association for the Advancement of Science, 1989), MDE officials together with MSTA and local educators revised the state's science objectives. One of the MDE's science coordinators explained: "The state's science objectives tie in very closely with Project 2061, Science for all Americans. When we were getting ready to develop the new objectives, Project 2061 had just been released . . . We saw that it was going to influence science education nationally and because of that the Michigan objectives were very closely aligned with that." Michigan's 1991 standards for science education were developed around "scientific literacy for all students" (Michigan State Board of Education, 1991).

A key component of "scientific literacy" involved transforming the science content that students learned. For state policymakers, reshuffling the scientific topics in the K–12 curriculum represented only the tip of the iceberg in reforming science education. They sought to shift the science curriculum from a mélange of isolated facts and information to a focus on understanding key scientific concepts. One MDE science coordinator commented that revising the state's objective was "based on the vision that science should be taught in greater depth with fewer concepts." The science coordinator contrasted this emphasis with conventional science education, which "was a quick kind of lesson that would change from day to day. I had sat in classes and observed teachers teach four or five different topics in one hour . . . The students learned nothing. They would memorize facts." The state's revised standards proposed that the knowledge necessary for scientific literacy should be organized around a few fundamental and interconnected ideas that had rich explanatory power. Another MDE science coordinator explained: "My understanding is more that students are able to make connections between the broad important ideas such as cellular respiration and other subject matter areas . . . That required spending more time with a topic area and therefore less content coverage."

A second dimension of scientific literacy pressed by state reformers involved teaching students to use scientific concepts and skills. Unlike the traditional science curriculum in which the use of science knowledge is rarely emphasized, state policymakers argued that knowing science required students to know how to use scientific knowledge. Committing scientific constructs to memory was simply not enough. They wanted students to use their knowledge to describe, explain, and predict scientific phenomena. Further, the state standards encouraged a science curriculum in which students engaged in scientific inquiry by developing questions as well as observing and measuring in experimental and naturally occurring situations to answer these questions. State policymakers wanted students to develop scientific "habits of mind" in order to understand connections between scientific inquiry and results. Moreover, the policymakers wanted students to justify and critique their findings and draw conclusions. The revised state objectives argue that K–12 students should learn to reflect on the limits and consequences of the science knowledge they generate through their scientific activity, just like professional scientists do.

State policymakers sought more than the infusion of extra scientific activities into the curriculum; the intent here was not to have students practice further the steps in the "scientific method" or engage in more cookbook experiments and other hands-on activities. One of the MDE's science coordinators explained,

> It seems to me that we've been doing a lot of hands-on science for a long time . . . A lot of teachers, . . . do the hands-on experiences and really like them and think "Oh, this is great science because students are really doing science and that's great." I think that's a nice first step, but I don't consider hands-on science in and of itself to be one of the ends. . . . Hands-on is in the service of something else, and that is conceptual understanding . . . so we need to take it to that next step.

State policymakers sought an approach to scientific inquiry in which students learned that doing science involved posing questions, justifying and critiquing findings, drawing conclusions, and reflecting on the limits and effects of these conclusions. State standards proposed replacing textbook-scripted, cookbook laboratory experiments with a more authentic notion of scientific inquiry. Finally, the standards argued that to be scientifically literate, students had to understand science in the real world, appreciating that scientific themes vary depending on their context in the natural and technological realms.

State standards also promoted a major transformation in the pedagogy of science education, toward an approach that was grounded in students' prior knowledge of scientific ideas: students were to develop new understandings of a scientific idea by reconstructing their existing knowledge of that idea. One of the MDE's science coordinators explained that the standards involved "Basing science education on students' understanding . . . constructivist and conceptual change models and then looking at delivery systems that really support that."

In contrast with the state's mathematics standards, the science standards elaborated on core ideas through brief essays that identified key concepts, terms, and tools for each objective as well as its "real-world" application. Organized around a few central questions, such essays described the development of students' understanding of key scientific ideas.

These mathematics and science standards sought tremendous changes in Michigan classrooms. The successful implementation of these ideas about mathematics and science education would involve much more than adding to, subtracting from, or shuffling around mathematics or science topics. The standards required a reconceptualization of science and mathematics education.

The Context of State Standards

Having wonderful ideas is one thing; getting others to heed those ideas is another matter. The challenges for state policymakers were immense. To begin with, state policymakers sought tremendous changes in existing classroom practices, changes that most teachers were ill-equipped to understand or carry out. The MDE's mathematics coordinator summed up the challenge when he remarked that the "average teacher teaching in Michigan had one mathematics course, most likely her undergraduate work, seventeen and a half years ago . . . We've got a lot of people who haven't had a real close connection with the latest developments in mathematics education."

Moreover, the new ideas about classroom practice, especially mathematics practice, were not well developed. The mathematics standards in particular were short on details with respect to how their new ideas would take shape in the classroom. Underspecified policies tend not to get implemented (Mazmanian and Sabatier, 1983).

There were other challenges. The MDE had few resources to support the implementation of its science and mathematics standards. Moreover, whatever resources the MDE had were spread out among a variety of independent units within the agency. In addition, standards were not the only game in the state's education policy agenda; a variety of other items, including charter schools, had found their way onto the policy agenda. Further, members of the MDE were still very conscious that they operated in a state where local control had been the standard operating procedure for years. There were some causes for optimism, most notably, new state policy initiatives substantially increased the clout of the state, especially the MEAP.

Policymaking on a Shoestring Budget

Like most state departments of education, the MDE was understaffed and underresourced. Downsizing initiatives and hiring freezes in the 1980s only exacerbated these matters. The MDE did not have the infrastructure to support the implementation of standards that pressed fundamental changes in mathematics and science education.

Persuasion was one means the MDE used to get school districts and schools to notice their standards. By involving a wide range of local educators and professionals in developing the standards, MDE officials hoped they would get local educators to buy in. According to one of the MDE's science coordinators, "I think because of the way we went about it—that is, going out into the trenches and involving a wide array of people and bringing people along and letting them have a stake in where we were going— eventually people felt that they were truly among the architects of this new document." Further, MDE officials spent considerable time giving presentations about the standards to local school districts and organizations around the state.

For MDE officials, aware of the state's local control ethos, presentations in local school districts were by local invitation only. As the MDE's mathematics consultant explained, "It's an awful lot of being invited on behalf of districts or organizations to go out and participate with whatever they're doing." One of the MDE's science coordinators commented, "Very seldom do we invite ourselves in . . . When you invite yourself in, teachers feel somehow threatened or that you're coming in to inspect." The MDE's mathematics consultant captured the situation noting, "Here at the Department of Education we don't endorse motherhood or apple pie, we're the local autonomy [state] . . . I think our role is to assist districts in whatever way is necessary." The MDE science and mathematics coordinators saw their role as providing assistance to school districts when requested rather than monitoring local implementation of the state standards.

Reliance on local school-district hospitality was not the only challenge. The magnitude of Michigan's education system, with its over eighty thousand teachers spread across 545 school districts, dwarfed the MDE; the MDE had one mathematics coordinator and two science coordinators. Further, the MDE relied mostly on either federal money or private foundation money to fund these positions. One science coordinator was funded entirely from private foundation and federal money, while the other was funded in large part by two federal programs—Title 1 of ESEA and Eisenhower Mathematics and Science Education Program. Over 50 percent of the mathematics coordinator position was paid from federal Title 1 and Eisenhower funds. As a result of these funding arrangements, these coordinators had to spend part of their time helping with the administration of federal programs. Moreover, both the mathematics and science coordinators had meager budgets to support any implementation efforts. The MDE's mathematics coordinator explained that his unit relied entirely on federal funding: "I don't have one at all. If the Eisenhower funds were taken from us, our little unit would dry up, it's that critical." "There's very little money if you want to provide staff development," the science coordinator remarked. "You have to go out and beat the bushes or beat somebody else's bush to make it happen . . . You don't have a budget to make that happen."

Three state coordinators could not single-handedly reform science and mathematics instruction in Michigan. Even if they had an abundance of funds, they were unlikely to reach more than a small fraction of Michigan's teachers. Making the most of their meager resources, they provided broad overviews of the standards to large gatherings of local educators. Describing these efforts as giving the "state of the state in science," one science coordinator went on to explain, "I get asked for updates and the big picture . . . We try to maximize our time by attending those functions where we impact a lot of people. It's not very cost effective for the department, or time effective for us, to go out and talk to three or four." When the MDE managed to reach administrators and teachers directly, it was only able to provide general overviews of the standards; these offerings were unlikely to be sufficient to support the local implementation of the instructional changes that the standards urged.

The MDE, then, could not reach many teachers and administrators directly; it could only affect them through other avenues. One such avenue was the state policy system.

Policy Instruments and Strategies

State policymakers mobilized a variety of policy instruments that MDE officials hoped would draw local educators' attention to state standards. Moreover, MDE officials worked to align their standards with other state policies, especially tying standards to the mandatory MEAP. With assistance from professional associations and local educators, the MDE revised the MEAP mathematics test in 1989 and the MEAP science test in 1996 to make them more consistent with state standards.

State officials acknowledged that their efforts at aligning the state's objectives with the MEAP tests were not an overwhelming success, at least not in mathematics. Part of the problem stemmed from the MDE's limited budget. One MDE official who was openly critical of the MEAP for mathematics and its reliance on multiple-choice items complained:

> After the state objectives were all laid out, by committee we said now given these objectives, what's the best way to assess them? And it came out one-third of these items in a multiple choice format; about one-third of the items really require some type of free response, even if it's very short (those tend to be the application kinds of questions); and about one-third of the items require performance and those tended to be the conceptual items. As push came to shove, [however,] basically financial push came to shove and we reduced those items to multiple choice.

Absent funds for developing and scoring open-ended and performance items, the MEAP ended up almost entirely multiple choice in format. Indeed, the extended-response items at the end of the test were, according to one MDE official, never scored because they were "so expensive and time consuming."

The difficulties of aligning the MEAP with state objectives were not entirely financial. The MEAP served at least two purposes. On the one hand, some of the state's mathematics and science reformers saw the MEAP as a potent tool for encouraging change in classroom instruction. Their concern was with the extent to which the MEAP items represented the sort of content and pedagogy they were pursuing through the state's objectives. On the other hand, the MEAP was not just a policy tool designed to move local practice in new directions. It was designed to measure how well students, schools, and school districts were doing. And, as one might expect, fairness was of utmost concern here. Fearful of lawsuits, the MDE's testing experts were concerned about the reliability of their questions and other psychometric properties of the test. Multiple-choice tests are much more reliable compared with difficult-to-score performance and open-ended tests. A state subject-matter coordinator remarked, "We've limited ourselves to these very unrealistic, inadequate forms of assessment, basically our standardized testing. When we try to break some of the mold there, I think that we hear far too often from measurement people that we can't do these things for the wrong reasons—we'll get sued." The "darn liability sorts of issues," as one MDE official put it, had the upper hand at least in the case of the mathematics MEAP.

As a predominantly multiple choice test, the revised MEAP for mathematics was not a mirror image of the state's mathematics objective; it failed to capture and represent the depth of the content and pedagogical changes pressed by the state's objectives. One MDE official claimed that over 90 percent of the MEAP items measured procedural mathematical knowledge. Hence, depending on whether they turned to the state's objectives or the MEAP, local administrators and teachers might have constructed rather different advice about mathematics education. Things were different for the MEAP for science, which was revised in the 1990s. Including both performance and constructed response questions, the MEAP for science more closely aligned with the state's science objectives.

Changes to state legislation in the early 1990s were intended to give the state's standards more clout. Public Act 25 (1990) changed the incentive structure for local districts by defining tangible sanctions (that is, loss of 5 percent of all state funds) for schools that failed to comply with the provisions of the act. Among other things, Public Act 25 required local schools to write and implement a school improvement plan and develop a curriculum in terms of student outcomes. In 1991, the same legislator who developed Public Act 25 mandated a high school proficiency test that was to be aligned with state standards (Public Act 118). Further, students who passed the test would receive a state-endorsed diploma as an inducement for students and parents to take the test seriously. And in 1993, Public Act 335 mandated "a required core academic curriculum for all school districts" and introduced new compliance mechanisms in the form of a summary school accreditation process. As interpreted by the MDE, the summary accreditation process required schools to meet explicit student performance provisions. Specifically, schools that failed to have 65 percent of their students score in the "satisfactory" range on MEAP tests would not receive state accreditation. Moreover, unaccredited schools would lose 5 percent of their state aid. This was a significant penalty considering that recent changes in state law had increased the state's share of school funding. The MEAP was the state's chief instrument for getting locals to pay attention to state standards, and the summary accreditation process was very likely to heighten its salience for local schools and school districts.

Public Act 25 (1990) aligned the state's school improvement and accreditation requirements with its standards for mathematics, science, and other subjects. MDE officials had also hitched their wagons to the systemic reform bandwagon. With federal funding designed to promote systemic reform, they worked to align their various initiatives on mathematics and science. One senior official described a "big push for connections, a big push for holistic thinking about school improvement." Another remarked, "I think the cohesive alignment of policy and practice is the major thrust of this department's policies and procedures in terms of how you bring that to bear on a district." The MDE had established bimonthly meetings for the purpose of making staff aware of each other's initiatives and, as one official put it, getting them to work "toward some common goals." But aligning the efforts of different MDE units and officials was difficult in practice. For example, according to one official the MDE's bimonthly meetings rarely went beyond "quick and dirty updates" and "superficial" exchanges. Another official wondered whether there were people in the MDE who knew what the mathematics and science standards were. He went on noting with respect to the standards, "I think we've gotten to the situation here where we have yet to discuss the basic philosophical issues."

Part of the challenge in aligning the MDE's mathematics and science initiatives stemmed from the different programs, frequently federal, operated by different MDE units that supported these initiatives. One official went so far as to say that "there's no coordination among any of these MDE walls . . . People are all over the place. There is a turf war." Another part of the challenge was resources. A subject-matter consultant noted: "The intent is for curriculum and assessment to work very closely together and the only reason why that may not happen as well as we would like to is because everybody is so busy. Everyone is so accustomed to trying to get the job done and having very little time to do it." Resource thin, MDE officials had insufficient time to get their own jobs done, let alone check in with colleagues in other units to make sure they were on the same page.

The resource shortage also undermined the MDE's ability to enforce its alignment efforts. Consider the MDE's attempts to promote greater alignment between state standards and professional development. MDE officials encouraged school districts to use the federal funds they were entitled to through the Eisenhower Mathematics and Science Education Program to support professional development about the state's standards. The MDE used the application review process for the Eisenhower Program to press districts to use this federal funding to build local capacity for implementing the standards. Thus, state policymakers used federal monies as an inducement for school districts. Aside from revising the proposals submitted by local school districts, however, the MDE lacked the staff to ensure that districts used this money to support professional development for implementing the state's standards.

A similar situation was evident with respect to the state-supported network of regional Mathematics and Science Centers, another potentially important source of professional development for local school districts. The state legislature provided additional funding for the network in 1993, enabling considerable expansion. But the MDE exercised only limited influence over the activities of these regional centers. As one observer of the system pointed out, whether these regional centers worked to support the implementation of state standards depended a lot on the "historical accident" of the expertise of people who staffed them. While the MDE vetted proposals for funding from each regional Mathematics and Science Center, it did not have the resources to oversee how these funds were used.

State Politics

State standards did not exist in a policy or political wilderness. Like all policies, they were grafted onto a state policy landscape that was cluttered with the fruits of policies past. Moreover, the standards movement did little to curtail state government's appetite for education policymaking. Standards-based reform resided in a volatile political context characterized by change, instability, and disharmony. Standards were not the only game in Lansing.

As education became increasingly politicized in the 1980s and 1990s, clashes emerged among different areas of state government—the legislature, the state board, and the executive and administrative branches. Democratic and Republican governors both sought to eliminate the State Board of Education. And during the mid-1990s, the situation really heated up. Republican governor Engler and the socially conservative Republican-controlled state board (1994–1996) were at odds over the appropriate role for state government in education. While the state board attempted to limit the MEAP, the governor worked to increase its clout. The MDE was caught in the middle. Critical of the MDE, Republican governor Engler oversaw significant reductions in the MDE's staffing and transferred responsibility from the MDE to other departments.

School choice initiatives also found their way onto the state policy agenda. In 1994, the Republican-controlled State Board of Education vigorously pressed charter schools and actively sought to make the state's "core curriculum" a model curriculum for schools rather than mandatory. While the Republican-controlled state board attempted to get rid of the mandated core curriculum, the Republican governor publicly supported the state's assessment system (MEAP). A senior MDE official remarked, "I think the governor has been . . . passively supportive of Goals 2000 [national standards], while at the same time overtly advancing charter schools." A revised school code (Public Act 289, 1996) defined the state's core curriculum as a model for local schools and enabled the expansion of charter schools by increasing the number of public school academies eligible for approval by universities. The revised school code, however, also held charter schools to the same accountability requirements as public schools.

These political tensions contributed to numerous changes in state policy between 1989 and 1996. While the substantive thrust of the state's objectives remained steady, the policy instruments and compliance procedures were in flux. Between 1990 and 1996, the state moved from a model core curriculum with incentives for local use to a mandated "academic core curriculum" (1993), and then back to a state core curriculum as a model for schools (1996). Each change brought new procedural requirements that local school districts had to meet to demonstrate compliance. While standards-based reform occupied a relatively central plank in Michigan's education policy agenda, there were also attempts to downsize the MDE, deregulate the state education bureaucracy, and promote a variety of school choice initiatives.

The Challenge for State Standards

State officials, aided by professional associations and local educators, made substantial progress in articulating and asserting their ideas about mathematics and science education. But their initiatives conflicted with a number of policymaking realities. First, they had to contend with the political realities of a system intentionally designed to frustrate and fragment coherent government. Second, state reformers had to persist in an unsettled political and policy environment. Third, in a state with a history of deference to local control they had to rely on the hospitality of local school districts. Fourth, they had to deal with the realities of scarce resources to support the implementation of their ideals.

Under these circumstances, it was unlikely that the state's mathematics and science standards would get very far without additional help. One potential source of assistance was the local school district. For state policymakers, getting local policymakers like Ann Smith on board was critical to the successful local implementation of the state's standards. Though constitutionally creatures of the state, by tradition school districts had a great deal of authority. Their assistance could not be taken for granted.

Analyzing the Progress of Standards in Local Practice

Gauging policy success is complex, in large part because it is hard to find reasonable criteria for noticing the standards in local school districts and schools. Absent some sort of gauge, it is difficult to take up the extent to which local school districts practiced in ways that resonated with the mathematics and science standards. This is a version of a perennial problem of implementation research—it is difficult to derive implementation indicators from vague and shifting policy goals (Linder and Peters, 1987; Winters, 1990). The complexity of gauging success increases considerably when the policy under investigation seeks fundamental changes in existing behavior. Because the policies are novel, educators and researchers have no clear sense of what sorts of change would constitute policy success.

As discussed earlier, Michigan's mathematics and science standards sought changes in what topics were taught, when they were taught, student grouping arrangements, and classroom materials, among other things. At their core, however, the standards advanced a fundamental refocusing of what counted as worthwhile mathematical and scientific knowledge, and what it meant to engage in doing mathematics and science in classrooms. Distinguishing between procedural and principled knowledge is helpful here. Procedural knowledge centers on computational procedures and mainly involves following predetermined steps to accurately compute correct answers. For example, elementary school students need to know an important piece of procedural knowledge: "Count the number of decimals at the right of the decimal point and then you put the decimal that number of places over" in order to multiply decimals. Although it constitutes only a part of the field of mathematics and science, procedural knowledge has dominated the K–12 curriculum (Romberg, 1983). By contrast, principled knowledge involves key concepts that are used to construct procedures for solving mathematical and scientific problems. In the multiplication of decimals example, principled knowledge would involve a firm grasp of place value and understanding that not only do numerals have a value, but their place has a value also. The standards pressed a curriculum that balanced principled and procedural knowledge.

For these ideas to be successfully implemented in local school systems, at least two dimensions of classroom instruction would have to change: the academic tasks that students work on and the discourse they engage in around these tasks. Academic tasks—the questions, problems, and exercises that students work on—form the "basic treatment unit" in classrooms and serve as the proximal cause of student learning from instruction (Doyle, 1983).

Drawing students' attention to particular aspects of content, academic tasks define the intellectual products that students are to produce and the approaches they are to take in doing so. The successful implementation of the mathematics and science standards would require academic tasks that balance principled knowledge with procedural knowledge.

Classroom discourse norms concern the ways in which teachers and students interact with each other and how they agree and disagree. Academic tasks as presented and set up by the teacher often undergo a substantial metamorphosis as they are played out and enacted by students and teacher (Doyle and Carter, 1984; Stein, Grover, and Henningsen, 1996). Discourse norms in a classroom can fundamentally transform an academic task from being mostly about principled knowledge to being all about procedural knowledge. If Michigan students were to gain an appreciation for mathematical and scientific inquiry as promoted by the standards, they would need opportunities to evaluate the truth of mathematical and scientific ideas, to reason aloud about their conjectures, and to learn how to defend and revise these conjectures.

Because my understanding of the mathematics and science standards centers on what counts as mathematics and science knowledge and inquiry, my gauge of successful implementation of the standards moves beyond an exclusive focus on the curricular materials, classroom activities, topic coverage, and student grouping arrangements. My gauge for the success focuses on the extent to which academic tasks and classroom discourse norms balance principled and procedural mathematics and science knowledge. This sort of gauge is important because teachers can adopt new materials and new instructional activities without ever changing the intellectual rigor of the mathematics and science content.

CHAPTER 3

Interactive Policymaking

Sonny naughton is enthusiastic about his work. His energy for improving education in rural Littleton is immense. His spacious if makeshift office over the high school gym, with numerous workstations piled high with everything from curricular materials to grant proposals, is testimony to that. As curriculum director for Littleton public schools, Naughton oversees instructional policy for the one thousand students who attend the district's high school, middle school, and sole elementary school. Littleton is a small, economically depressed, predominantly white, rural town. The district's central office administration consists of a superintendent, a curriculum director, and six support staff. Naughton juggles multiple roles—including writing grants to supplement the district's operating budget, facilitating instructional policymaking for the school district, monitoring improvement efforts and student achievement, overseeing the implementation of an array of new programs, coordinating services between the school district and other social service agencies, and purchasing curricular materials.

Multiple hats, ill health, and a paucity of resources have not dampened Naughton's zeal for improving education in Littleton public schools. Sixteen-hour days and seven-day weeks are often necessary to manage the ambitious reform agenda he has pieced together, one that addresses everything from classroom instruction to student health. With financial and technical support from government and private-sector competitive grants, Naughton has spearheaded district efforts to reform mathematics and science education. Recently, Littleton successfully competed for federal funds to support reforming mathematics and science education and also received a quarter of a million dollars from a private foundation to implement an integrated services program for at-risk students. Aided by committees of teachers and administrators, Naughton has revised district policies on mathematics and science education.

Naughton saw the state's mathematics and science standards as an asset, not an imposition. He used the standards, especially the state's MEAP test, as a template for Littleton's mathematics and science policies. Committees of teachers and administrators wrote district curriculum guidelines that mirrored the state's standards. Further, Sonny Naughton used the state standards to augment the authority of school-district policies with teachers and school administrators, or, as he put it, as a "hammer" to drive change in classroom instruction. Using MEAP data he identified areas in the curriculum where students were not performing well and then worked with teachers to redress these problems. While the state standards played a central role in district policymaking in Littleton, Naughton and his colleagues also turned to other sources to inform their instructional policymaking, including private consultants, textbook publishers, and national standards, most notably NCTM.

Serving a working-class white rural town, the Riverville public school system is recognized across the state for its efforts to revise mathematics education. Linda Burton, Riverville's director of curriculum, and Lisa Carter, a mathematics teacher at the district's sole middle school, were the primary movers and shakers in these efforts. In a small district office made up of a superintendent and a curriculum director, Burton and Carter, together with a cadre of lead teachers, had worked for almost a decade to transform mathematics education for the two thousand students enrolled in Riverville public schools. State standards were not the primary motivator for Burton and Carter. In dire financial straights in the early 1980s, Riverville decided to focus on improving instruction and its administrator sought outside sources of financial and technical support for these efforts. Working through the local intermediate school district, Burton and Carter successfully competed for federal Eisenhower grant money to fund an ambitious professional development program in mathematics for teachers. They hoped to transform mathematics education in the district from the bottom up by building teacher capacity to teach mathematics. They also courted assistance from mathematics and education scholars at a local university. They offered to pilot new mathematics curricula for the university, while in return receiving from the university technical assistance and expertise about improving mathematics instruction. Work by the National Council of Teachers of Mathematics was also an important source of guidance for Carter and Burton.

By the time state policymakers had put their mathematics standards in print, Riverville's leaders were already harnessed to the mathematics reform bandwagon. Still, the state's mathematics standards were not lost on them. While Burton and other administrators found the state's "quick-fix mandates" a nuisance at times, distracting them from their established long-term reform agenda, they acknowledged that state standards helped focus their efforts, justifying their push for a common approach to mathematics instruction across Riverville's classrooms. Further, the state's mathematics standards served as a hammer, especially for school principals, to move some reluctant teachers in the instructional reform direction advanced by Riverville's mathematics policies. The principal of Riverville Middle School put it most directly, noting that state policy "is a motivating force and a strong one."

Redwood public schools serves a mid-sized rust belt city. Of the 25,000 students enrolled in the district, more than half come from low-income families and about half are African American. Like many urban school districts, Redwood's district office is a sprawling affair with responsibility for instructional policy farmed out among an array of subunits, including an assessment office, a school improvement and staff development office, a mathematics office, a science office, and a compensatory education office. Rhonda Burlington, an energetic middle-aged woman and twenty-five-year veteran of the district, works as a mathematics instructional specialist in the compensatory education office that is responsible for the federal Title 1 program for the district. She is very knowledgeable about mathematics and mathematics education and deeply enthusiastic about improving mathematics education, especially for poor students. A leader in the state's Council of Teachers of Mathematics and well connected in the mathematics community nationally, Burlington was very proud of her accomplishments as a woman in an association where men have held most of the leadership positions. Burlington was also an active member of the state-level committee that developed the state's mathematics standards.

Burlington and the compensatory education office, rather than the district's mathematics office, led efforts to revise Redwood's mathematics program, which had remained stagnant for twenty years. She remarked that as "president of the Michigan Council of Teachers in Mathematics . . . I had the ability to bring back a lot of firsthand knowledge. And that's when compensatory education decided that we would be a real spearhead in this district to bring the new directions in mathematics from the state and the national level here." Indeed, using federal Title 1 funds Burlington provided extensive professional development for compensatory education teachers on new approaches to mathematics education—before the state standards made it off the printing presses. She had even managed to provide access to these workshops for some regular classroom teachers. After a number of false starts, Burlington managed to convince Redwood's board of education that the district's mathematics program was in need of a major overhaul. Handpicking a committee of teachers "who in the last five years had shown a lot of openness to the new direction in math," she worked with the district's mathematics coordinator to rewrite the district's policies about mathematics education. As one might expect given Burlington's involvement with writing the state's mathematics standards, the state standards were especially influential in these local policymaking efforts.

Casting state and federal agencies in policymaking roles, policy analysts often focus their work on the extent to which local school districts like Littleton, Riverville, and Redwood implement the policies of state and federal agencies. Few implementation analysts consider the school district as a policymaking entity in its own right. But school districts like Littleton, Riverville, and Redwood were making instruction policy, not just carrying out the state's policy directives. Taking a policymaking stance, district officials like Burlington and Burton defined policy problems and developed their own policies about mathematics and science education. In making district policy, these local officials used a variety of sources for ideas and guidance, including but not limited to state policy. State and local school-district relations on matters of instruction involved an interactive policymaking process.

The School District and Instructional Policy

School districts like Riverville and Redwood had made instructional policy for a decade or more. These school districts did not cease making policy as state policymaking activity increased. District officials like Burlington and Burton made sense of state policy initiatives as makers of local policies about instruction rather than as implementers of state policies.

Instructional policymaking was a relatively recent pursuit for most school districts in the study, an activity that most had taken up in the past quarter-century. The "back-to-basics" movement of the 1970s and early 1980s prompted five of the school districts to pay greater attention to instructional issues and attempt to influence classroom instruction through various combinations of policy instruments, including curriculum guides, student assessment, instructional supervision, curriculum materials, and professional development. Making instructional policy represented a significant departure for these school districts, which had traditionally left to the schools instructional decisions such as the choice of curricular materials. Desegregation attempts were also a motivating factor in Redwood and Hamilton, the two larger urban districts. While these two districts had made instructional policy for more than a half-century, instructional policymaking accelerated in the late 1970s as district officials attempted to standardize curricula across schools.

The larger school districts had more instructional policies and more elaborate systems for monitoring their implementation. By the early 1980s, for example, suburban Parkwood had enacted numerous policies about instruction that focused on textbooks, student assessment, staff development, curriculum guidelines, and teacher evaluation. Similarly, by 1987, urban Hamilton had established a system for monitoring classroom instruction that detailed for teachers what skills to teach, acceptable levels of mastery, and strategies for reteaching particular skills. Designed to ensure that teachers complied with district policies, this system required teachers to record, on district-provided monitoring sheets, students' scores on end-of-unit tests. Teachers turned in these monitoring sheets to the principal, who reviewed them periodically with district officials. For smaller districts like Littleton and Lakeside, involvement with instructional policymaking had more recent origins, prompted in good measure by the increased state policy activity of the 1980s.

With the exception of rural Woodland, school districts took a proactive policymaking stance on instructional matters, responding to increased state policymaking by developing their own local instructional policies. The state's expanding role in instructional policymaking did not dampen these local school districts' enthusiasm for policymaking. Indeed, in most districts the state's policy initiatives supplied occasions for more district policymaking.

State and district policies offered guidance about similar aspects of instruction. Both broadcast signals to teachers about what they should be doing in their classrooms. Relations between state and local government, then, involved interactions between two independent instructional policymaking arenas—that is, it involved interactive policymaking. For the purpose of analyzing the school district's response to state policy, the interactive policymaking perspective has at least three advantages. First, using an interactive policymaking perspective, district officials are viewed not merely as doers of higher-level policy, but also as policymakers in their own right. Having access to various sources for ideas about addressing these problems, they assess the merits of these ideas through deliberations with colleagues, craft these ideas into policy proposals, and work to get teachers and school administrators to adopt them. According to this view, district officials play an array of roles that would remain largely hidden from an implementation perspective. Second, the interactive policymaking perspective complicates relations between state policy and the local school district because it suggests that state or federal policy can influence what school districts do in and through the district policymaking process. District officials' work vis-à-vis state policy is not nearly as straightforward as putting into practice state policymakers' decisions. Third, whereas state or federal policy is front and center in the implementation perspective, in the interactive policymaking perspective it becomes one of a number of potential sources that district officials use as they craft local policy about instruction.

The School District Policy Process

If state and local government relations are characterized as interactive policymaking, then it behooves us to examine the district policymaking process. It is by understanding who the central actors are in the district policymaking process, what policy instruments they use, and where they turn for advice that we can begin to unpack the local response to state and national standards.

The Prominence of Education Professionals and Specialists

Professional educators like Littleton's Sonny Naughton and Redwood's Rhonda Burlington, rather than elected officials, parents, and community elites, were the chief instructional policymakers in the nine school districts. District and school administrators, curriculum specialists, and teachers crafted district instructional policy. Local school boards adopted a mostly perfunctory stance. A rural board member summed up the situation: "In the twelve years that I've been on the school board, all twelve years' worth of meetings, you'd probably put academic issues into two or three meetings." While the local school board approved new instructional policies and in some cases authorized the revision of existing policies, professional educators were typically the ones who worked out issues about mathematics and science education. Another rural school board member captured the situation, noting: "We've had several teacher curriculum committees and they bring the recommendations to the school improvement team. Usually the recommendations that come out of there come to the board, and there's very few times that we don't approve." An urban board member talking about her district's policies on mathematics education remarked, "We're messing around with the Chicago math program. I'm not sure what that is . . . I don't know if it's all the buildings or not. I think it's not, but I don't know." Considered the most knowledgeable about instruction on her school board, she lamented the inattention to issues of instruction: "Teaching and learning are probably the kind of stuff we ought to be talking about at board meetings rather than how much per square inch it costs to scrape asbestos off the ceiling beams. But it's a whole lot easier to zero in on scraping asbestos off than it is to look at broad concepts about teaching and learning." Parents and the larger community were further removed from the school district's mathematics and science policymaking process.

There were some exceptions to this pattern. In the two more affluent suburban school districts, for example, parents and the school board became engaged in the instructional policymaking process when controversial changes were proposed that went beyond the "zone of tolerance" of local elites (Boyd, 1976). In suburban Parkwood and Pleasant Valley, a group of parents became engaged in instructional policymaking when the district office developed policies to get rid of ability-based tracking in the high school and middle school. In both districts, the detracking policy initiatives went against the expectations of some elite parents who were concerned about their children's chances of admission to prestigious colleges, and they mobilized others to oppose the policy. Putting pressure on the local school boards, these parents managed to scuttle these policy initiatives in one district and put them on hold in the other. Parent participation in the policymaking process was more reactive than proactive (see also Kirst and Walker, 1971). Still, parents' reactive engagement had definite consequences for the school district's instructional policies.

In the larger urban and suburban school districts, district-office science or mathematics specialists took responsibility for instructional policymaking initiatives. Working with committees of teachers and school administrators, who were often hand-picked, they crafted policies about mathematics and science education. In these districts, senior district-office administrators, even those with responsibility for curriculum (for example, the director of curriculum and assistant superintendent for curriculum) tended to defer to the subject matter specialist on the particulars of mathematics and science education policy. When asked about the district's science education policy, the curriculum director in a suburban district responded: "It is Tina's [the district-office science education specialist's] ball game . . . We just leave Tina alone . . . She is the science person here, frankly, and that's what we all know and agree to." Another senior administrator remarked when asked about the substantive thrust of the district's science education policy, "Tina can go into that at length." Subject matter specialists took the lead in determining the substance of district policies about science and mathematics education.

In smaller school districts like Lakeside and Riverville, regular classroom teachers took leadership roles in making instructional policy, usually with the help of committees of fellow teachers. In rural Lakeview, for example, Ann Smith, a full-time middle-school teacher, took responsibility for developing policies about science education. The superintendent of rural Woodland delegated responsibility for science and mathematics education policymaking to two full-time teachers who also served as the district's mathematics and science coordinators. With respect to mathematics, he remarked: "I'm familiar with mathematical problem solving through Carl [a full-time teacher and mathematics coordinator]. Carl is a member of the National Council of Teachers of Mathematics, also the Michigan Teachers of Mathematics Association. He goes to all of those meetings . . . Anybody's got a math problem in this school district, talk to Carl." While administrators in rural Riverville were active in efforts to develop policies about mathematics education, Lisa Carter, the middle-school teacher, was in the driving seat. District and school administrators openly acknowledged as much. The junior high principal summed up the situation noting, "Lisa was so important . . . she really got the drift of things and charged out in front. She talked about things that had to happen with kids as a result of teaching." In some smaller districts, senior administrators delegated responsibility for mathematics and science policy to teachers or continued to play an active role but left teachers to take the lead.

The Central Role of Nongovernment Agents and Agencies

Instructional policymaking in the school district was informed by an array of sources—including, but not limited to, state policy. Ann Smith, who spearheaded rural Lakeside's policymaking efforts for science education, explained: "We drew curriculum from all of the nation. We wrote letters and we had the Kellogg grant, and also . . . other districts' and other states' curriculum documents. California and Wisconsin were two of the states that we relied heavily on." For ideas, technical assistance, materials, and money, Riverville's Linda Burton and Lisa Carter turned to faculty at a neighboring university, the National Council of Teachers of Mathematics, and the federal Eisenhower grant program, among other sources. District policymakers in seven of the nine school districts took advice on instruction from multiple sources, many of them beyond the formal education governance system. State policymakers did not have a monopoly on the ideas that informed district instructional policymaking. Further, to support their policy development and implementation efforts they drew on material and financial resources from a variety of sources, including private foundations.

Professional associations and networks were especially important. Rhonda Burlington's efforts to revise mathematics policies in urban Redwood were motivated and informed by her involvement with the Michigan Council of Teachers of Mathematics (MCTM). Similarly, district-level efforts to revise mathematics education in suburban Parkwood were supported in important ways by the involvement of district policymakers in MCTM. The mathematics coordinator in suburban Pleasant Valley identified the NCTM standards as especially influential in his efforts to develop policy about mathematics education. He explained: "The NCTM standards were coming out at the same time, in '89, and so we had the opportunity to talk a lot about the standards within our district mathematics committee . . . So it had an impact on what we did; it just did not have the impact on starting it because we were going to start it anyway."

Although not the impetus for revising Pleasant Valley's mathematics policy, the NCTM standards were an important source for ideas in the policymaking process. Underscoring the importance of professional associations, the mathematics coordinator in this suburban district noted: "I've been a member of NCTM for over thirty-five years and I kind of find it hard to be in math education and not be one . . . Now, we've had people from our district that have had involvement with MCTM and NCTM activities . . . there's been some connection there . . . For example, I was at the MCTM Executive Board Meeting last Saturday and the state mathematics consultant was discussing the curriculum frameworks—the new thing that's out. I had my district mathematics group together Monday night and discussed it with them." Professional networks, coupled with the connections they often afforded district officials to state policymakers, provided access to ideas about instruction and a heads-up on where the state was going next with its instructional policies.

In rural Riverville, the NCTM standards as well as two mathematics educators from a neighboring university were especially influential in that district's policymaking about mathematics instruction. In suburban Pleasant Valley, the science coordinator reported that involvement with the National Science Resources Board and the National Science Teachers Association were critical in revising that district's policies about science education. For school-district policymakers, professional associations and networks were an especially influential conduit for ideas about reforming mathematics and science education. Indeed, in the five districts with reputations for instructional innovation, this conduit was more influential than state policy documents.

Nongovernmental agencies not only provided district policymakers with access to ideas about instruction; they also at times provided a variety of other resources such as funding and curricular materials that were important for the development and implementation of district instructional policy. To understand district instructional policymaking, it is necessary to look beyond the formal school governance system to agents and agencies including the NCTM, MCTM, neighboring universities, the Michigan Partnership for New Education's Frameworks Project, the National Science Foundation, the Kellogg Foundation, and private consultants. District officials combined these with sources inside the education system, including the Michigan Department of Education's curriculum projects, the state's regional Mathematics and Science Centers, and state policy documents. In crafting policy, district policymakers relied on many of the same sources for ideas about instruction as did state policymakers.

Staying Ahead by Being in the Know

While all districts had access to state policy via policy documents such as the state's Essential Goals and Objectives, some had earlier and more direct access than others. By virtue of participating in state instructional policymaking committees, some district officials were well versed in the new directions long before the state's policy documents hit the printing presses. This was especially evident in the two suburban districts, two rural districts, and one urban district. A suburban curriculum director explained that "Basil [the district mathematics coordinator] also sits on the state-level committees, understands where we are headed. So we are kind of a step ahead, and keep focused in those areas." Some districts, by virtue of their participation in the development of state instructional policy and their access to state department officials in general through professional networks, had a competitive edge or perhaps an unfair advantage over other districts not directly involved with state policymaking and policymakers. A suburban mathematics coordinator candidly acknowledged as much, noting, "It's very important to be a member, you know, to be involved with the state and the national if you can . . . I've had a connection there so I can bring things back." Districts in the know by virtue of their connections with the state policy arena were working on the development of district policies that supported and surpassed state policy even before the state policy documents were issued. Wanting to generate the best policies possible, state policymakers, with limited resources and capacity, rely on local educators to help them craft state policies. They turn to individuals who have expertise in mathematics and science education and who have reputations for doing innovative work. Hence, those locals who are already ahead of the curve are further advantaged by virtue of their involvement in the state policy process.

Parallel Policymaking

School districts also developed "generic" or subject-matter-neutral policies about instruction that cut across subject areas. These policies pressed changes in instruction that included the "middle-school concept," "outcomes-based education," "peer coaching," and "authentic assessment." Often more senior district officials, including curriculum directors and assistant superintendents, took the lead on these initiatives. The development of these policies tended to be parallel with the development and implementation of subject-matter-specific policies, a somewhat unusual circumstance given that both sets of policies targeted classroom instruction.

Responsibility for school-district education policymaking in general, and instructional policymaking in particular, was often segmented, especially in larger districts. In segmented organizations, "each person, each department, each level has only a part of any problem and no assumed need to worry about any other part" (Kanter, 1983, p. 29). Responsibility for instructional policy in Redwood and Hamilton, for example, was spread out across four or five different units of the district office. These segmented arrangements contributed to the development of an array of different district policies about instruction that, although not necessarily contradictory, were not monolithic in terms of their advice to teachers. Different subunits of the district office took the lead on different instructional policies, leaving teachers and school administrators to figure out whether and how this mélange of instruction policies might be integrated into a coherent approach. A district mathematics coordinator remarked: "We've had in the last five years or so a lot of things happen . . . not all necessarily bad. It's just that there are fifteen things coming at teachers at the same time . . . If you get too many positive things happening to you, you're overwhelmed." In addition to revising policies on mathematics and science instruction, subunits of Redwood's district office had also put in place policies that pressed outcomes-based education, cooperative learning, alternative assessment, and site-based management. The volume of district policy initiatives was considerable.

Federal and state policies contributed to the horizontal segmentation of the district office. As discussed in Chapter 1, segmentation is in part a product of "fragmented centralization"; federal and state funding for education expanded through numerous independent programs, each with its own channels for distributing funds and advice (Meyer and Scott, 1983; Rowan, 1982). Each program generated new revenues and defined new work for school districts. Districts dealt with these fragmented programs by developing segmented organizational structures to administer each program (Cohen, 1982; Meyer, Scott, and Strang, 1987). The superintendent of rural Lakeside captured the situation by noting: "Fragmentation is a biggie and this is where state and federal policies really help create fragmentation. I have all these little parts and pieces, and money now is being doled out to schools heavy in grants and grants come with their own little package and their own little overhead and their own little structure." Not only did these arrangements increase the administrative burden for district policymakers, they also contributed to parallel policymaking.

The School District's Policy Instruments

District policymakers deployed various combinations of policy instruments to support the implementation of their policies, including curricular frameworks, curricular materials, student assessment, instructional monitoring, and professional development. Curriculum guides, curricular materials, and professional development were the most popular instruments with school districts.

Curriculum Guides and Curricular Materials. Seven of the nine school districts devoted considerable resources to developing and regularly revising their curriculum guides for mathematics and science. (Two rural school districts purchased their guides from neighboring school districts.) Curriculum guides varied across districts in terms of their focus and degree of elaboration. The curriculum guides developed by some districts focused mainly on outlining what content was to be taught, typically in terms of student learning objectives for each grade or cluster of grades. The following are representative examples:

"Tell, show, and write time to the nearest half hour."
"Solve problems to find length, perimeter and volume."
"Identify sources of drinking water."

Other school districts, three in particular, developed curriculum guides that also offered advice on how the content might be taught to students and on students' misconceptions about a particular topic. Moreover, these curriculum guides were more elaborate, including lists of vocabulary to be taught to students, suggesting ways of connecting these objectives to real-world contexts beyond the classroom, and listing key concepts connected with these objectives. For example, suburban Pleasant Valley's curriculum guide for elementary science not only detailed the content to be covered, but also offered teachers suggestions about ways of approaching the content and what students typically understand about the subject matter. Pleasant Valley's seventh-grade curriculum guide for science, which filled two five-inch binders, specified precisely what information and skills students were to learn and how this material might be taught.

School districts also used curricular materials to support the implementation of their policies, typically selecting a commercially produced mathematics or science textbook that covered the material detailed in their curriculum guide. Two of the nine school districts, however, had developed their own curricular materials for science rather than relying on commercially produced materials. Suburban Pleasant Valley and rural Lakeview, for example, had developed an elaborate series of instructional units for science and had put together kits of lessons and materials for each unit that corresponded directly to the learning objectives outlined in their curriculum guides.

Professional Development. Professional development was an important policy instrument in all nine school districts. District officials, however, mobilized this policy instrument in distinctly different ways.

More than 80 percent of those district officials who had responsibility for professional development supported a transmission view of professional development. External consultants, district specialists, and teachers with specialized knowledge transmitted knowledge about instruction to classroom teachers in a "show and tell" manner. One district official described the approach: "It is my job to give workshops within the district . . . to demonstrate how teachers can use these manipulatives, what they can do with them in their classes. We go into classrooms for demonstration lessons with the students so that teachers can see." Telling, showing, and modeling were ways of transmitting alternative instructional approaches to teachers.

For these district policymakers, professional development involved a broad spectrum of topics, including content knowledge, pedagogical knowledge, training in generic teaching strategies, and knowledge of materials such as manipulatives, graphing calculators, and computers. If these topics were integrated at all, it was at a very general level. The result was a fragmented curriculum for teacher development in most districts. A district policymaker explained: "Teachers are going through outcome-based education. They are learning how to set up learning centers. They're learning how to do cooperative learning and [are receiving] a lot of staff development on developmental-appropriate practice." Knowledge about instruction often reflected on the specialization of the external professional development providers, on whom districts relied. It was left to teachers to master the different pieces and put them together in their day-to-day practice. For these district officials, motivating teachers to learn and change typically involved a combination of rewards and sanctions. A district official noted, "Teachers will be monitored . . . If the curriculum isn't monitored, it isn't taught." Another district official observed, "The state is going to be monitoring the success rate on the state's proficiency test. If students do not receive endorsed diplomas, it is going to come right back to 'Where was the teacher teaching this, and when?'" The monitoring of instruction, state assessment instruments, and the allocation of resources such as materials and money for professional development were among the primary sanctions and rewards that district officials used to motivate teachers to learn and change.

Fewer than 20 percent of the district officials, mostly those involved with rural Riverville's efforts to revise mathematics education, supported an alternative perspective on professional development. These district officials believed that teachers themselves should be key agents in their own learning, and they accorded a central role to teacher leaders in the facilitation of this process. External experts were important, but not as the sole or primary suppliers of instructional knowledge. Ongoing discussions among teachers, administrators, and external experts were viewed as occasions for grappling with the meaning of state and national standards, especially what these ideas might mean for classroom practice. Linda Burton, Riverville's curriculum director, noted, "As a classroom teacher, when my door is closed, I do what I want to, and that's the culture we're trying to change. No, we teachers and administrators are a community of learners just like your classroom is a community of learners." Fostering dialogue on ideas about instruction among teachers was at the core of professional development.

For these district officials, the curriculum for teacher development involved not only state and national standards and professional development workshops, but also the curricular materials teachers used, teachers' instructional practice, and students' work. Day-to-day classroom practice was a core element of professional development. Knowledge about instruction then was not a commodity imported from the outside into classrooms, because it was constructed through conversations among teachers, administrators, and external experts. The curriculum for teacher professional development was spread across students' work, national standards, classroom curricular materials, and teachers' attempts to implement the standards in their practice. In stark contrast with the majority perspective on professional development, teacher development was integrated around teachers' attempts to put the standards into practice. Burton summed up the situation: "We don't bring in this speaker one year and another speaker another year . . . We try to have an ongoing project. We've been doing the math portion for seven years, now . . . and what we try to do is work with a group of teachers at one time. We bring them in for two weeks, use a model unit—curriculum unit—and do training on that." For Burton and her colleagues, teachers' motivation to learn and change involved developing and sustaining teachers' identities as experts and learners with one another. An administrator stated, "We have strong teacher leaders in mathematics in each of our buildings . . . who push reform all the time. That is one huge factor." Creating a critical mass of teacher leaders who convinced other teachers that the new ideas about mathematics education were important for students was understood as crucial for instructional change.

School-District Policymaking and State Policy

Getting the attention of local educators through public policy can be difficult. Locals often pay no heed to state and federal policies (Firestone, 1989; Fullan, 1991; McLaughlin, 1987, 1990). But district officials like Sonny Naughton, Linda Burton, and Rhonda Burlington did not ignore the mathematics and science standards. To the contrary, they heeded the standards, albeit some more than others, and did everything they could to develop district policies that supported the ideas they understood from and about the standards.

To understand how state policy featured in district policymaking, we need to investigate how district policymakers made sense of state policy in the context of their district policymaking. Sense-making involves noticing and categorizing signals or cues from the environment; sense-makers "generate" or author the signals that they interpret (Weick, 1995). That district policymakers noticed and responded to state policy is not nearly as interesting as how they noticed the standards and what they noticed about them. The state standards took various forms, including the state's Essential Goals and Objectives, the MEAP, and state-sponsored professional development.

State standards were influential in the district policymaking process. They spurred district policymakers to revise, or develop for the first time, policies that defined and sequenced the mathematics and science topics that students were to learn. Districts gave a lot of attention to state policies, especially the MEAP and the state's Essential Goals and Objectives. Further, they reported that their attention had increased in recent years, especially in response to state mandates like core curricula that had tangible sanctions for noncompliance, such as loss of 5 percent of state aid. A small-town administrator's remarks were representative: "Anyone who says the MEAP doesn't have an impact is not being honest. Superintendents are made and broken based on the MEAP, and if you don't think superintendents put pressure on principals who in turn put pressure on people, you are mistaken." Even in suburban Pleasant Valley, where district policymakers reported that prior to the early 1990s they had paid little attention to state instructional policies, the state policy was very salient. When asked about major issues confronting the district, eleven of the thirteen Pleasant Valley district policymakers interviewed named the state's MEAP test as a major focus.

The sense that district policymakers made of state standards was influenced by their situation, especially their histories as instructional policymaking agencies. State standards were especially influential in the three districts that previously had no district mathematics and science policies. Policymakers in these districts reported that state standards pushed them to develop instructional policies. One official explained: "The state probably got us going a little sooner. We definitely needed it because there was nothing. If a new teacher came in there really wasn't anything other than a textbook . . . that was the curriculum." An administrator in another district remarked, "The one good thing about Public Act 25 was that it made everybody stop and look at the K–12 program."

State policy was an impetus for revising existing policies in the other six districts that had mathematics and science policies already in place in the early 1990s. State standards were an occasion for district policymaking, prompting these districts to revise their existing policies. A rural policymaker remarked: "The MEAP test certainly is one of the areas that we want to try to do better on. And one of the things that I've done too is try to examine the MEAP test and determine what areas of mathematics or science we haven't done well in and try to deal with that." Another policymaker remarked, "MEAP is consuming the district totally and completely . . . our whole curriculum is driven by this MEAP." In these districts, officials often understood state policy initiatives as legitimating their existing instructional policies. A suburban curriculum director explained: "I really support Public Acts 25, 335, and 339 because I think they match up with what I think is right to do for kids. I think they are providing a system for getting things done that are already happening here." The same district's mathematics coordinator echoed this sentiment, noting that state standards would involve mostly some tweaking of the district's existing policies: "I don't think this framework is going to turn us inside out or make us do a whole lot of things differently. I think what it's going to do is let us organize some things that we have a little better."

According to district officials, state sanctions were especially influential in motivating them to develop or revise their instructional policies to support the state's mathematics and science standards. Most district officials constructed the state policy environment by singling out the summary accreditation process and the MEAP, the key mechanism for determining accreditation status. A rural principal noted, "Now they've tied accreditation in with MEAP—65 percent or better of your children must achieve satisfactory on the MEAP—we will spend a whole lot more time pushing the type of things that are on the MEAP test." State sanctions figured prominently in district policymakers' sense-making.

But if state sanctions put pressure on school districts to change, it was also a pressure that empowered district policymakers. District policymakers used state sanctions to leverage change and boost the authority of their own policies with teachers and school administrators. In Lakeside, state sanctions and national standards were essential to Ann Smith's efforts to revise and implement new policies about science education. She explained: "The state mandates help. I mean, I know you can't legislate from the top down but boy, did it help those of us working at the absolute root level to say this is just not our philosophy being pushed on you but there are some mandates for change coming out nationally and statewide, I mean, it's hard for people to ignore the experience and the research that's backing up some of the changes that are occurring . . . We couldn't have done it without all of these guidelines."

Smith elaborated, noting how state policy was especially important for those teachers who were slow to change because they hoped that this policy effort too might pass: "It added pressure. We had already started our reform effort and I guess what it might have done [was encourage] some of the people who thought 'This is going to blow over. Let's just wait it out.' I think eventually everybody started to see that the blowing over isn't occurring." District policymakers used state policy to add clout to their district policies about instruction.

In arguing that district policymakers attended carefully to state standards, I am not implying that each local policymaker read the state's standards. I did not measure district officials' exposure to particular state policy documents. Such an approach would have been problematic because district officials rarely encountered standards exclusively through the packages disseminated by state policymakers. As shown earlier, district officials encountered these ideas in a variety of arenas and formats, including state policy texts and other publications, national reform documents, professional development workshops, professional meetings, conversations with colleagues, and popular education journals. State policy documents were part of a broader conversation about revising mathematics and science education that was enabled by a variety of agents, agencies, and mechanisms, both inside and outside the education system.

Interactive Policymaking and the Progress of Standards

From an interactive policymaking perspective, local implementation of standards concerned the extent to which district policies supported the ideas about reforming mathematics and science education pressed by those standards. As I will show in Chapter 6, the school district's instructional policies about mathematics and science education were the extent of many teachers' encounters with the state's standards. District policy became the state and national standards for most teachers.

Increased state policymaking was accompanied by more district policymaking. From the perspective of state policymakers, the crucial question was whether and to what extent district policies supported their attempts to revise mathematics and science education. Whether and to what extent district policies supported state and national standards depended on the particular aspect of the reform message and on the particular school district. As discussed in Chapter 2, classroom instruction is a multifaceted practice that includes content coverage, materials, teaching strategies, and ways of treating students' ideas. State and national standards sought changes in all of these facets of mathematics and science instruction. Yet standards were more influential on district policymaking for some facets of instruction than others, and their influence varied by district.

The Reach of Standards

At one level, state policy had a very powerful and uniform effect on the district policymaking process. District instructional policies specified mathematics and science topics for the K–12 curriculum and the sequencing of topic coverage in ways that were closely aligned with state standards. Littleton's Sonny Naughton described the process: "Basically, we identified the state's essential goals and objectives. We identified where they were on the MEAP —at which grade level and at which emphasis they were placed on the MEAP at those grade levels." Suburban Pleasant Valley's mathematics coordinator described a similar process: "What we did was to take all of the things that we were teaching that we thought were still important, and we pasted them up on the wall. And we took the MEAP objectives and we pasted them up with them in those categories to make sure that there weren't pieces of content that we were missing that MEAP suggested." Another suburban district policymaker explained:

> We have to make sure that we've got the right things at the right grades. We've had a situation before where if it was tested in fourth grade in September by the MEAP and we taught it in April in fourth grade, truthfully we didn't worry a whole lot about it . . . The MEAP scores didn't matter so much. Well, you'd better believe that's going to move to third grade now. We can't wait until April of fourth grade if it's tested in September of fourth grade.

State policy had become especially influential in determining topic coverage and sequencing in district policies. Seven school districts had developed curriculum guides, and two districts had purchased curriculum guides that closely matched the topic coverage and sequencing outlined by state policy.

With respect to topic coverage and sequencing, then, district policies provided strong support for state and national standards initiatives. In this sense, Michigan's state standards initiatives were a great success because local policymakers were using the advice that state and national reformers were pressing on topic coverage to craft district policies. Moreover, this support was consistent across districts; district policies were markedly similar in the messages they communicated to schools about mathematics and science topic coverage and sequencing. State standards had a relatively uniform influence on district policymaking, with district policies amplifying this aspect of the state's message about reforming mathematics and science education.

School-district policies also supported other aspects of the state's mathematics and science standards, though not nearly as prominently or as faithfully as topic coverage and sequencing. For example, the school districts pressed problem solving in their curriculum guides for mathematics and through their professional development programs. Similarly, school district policies urged teachers to engage their students in the scientific process. What district policies encouraged under these rubrics, however, was not always consistent with what was intended by state and national reformers.

The Uneven Progress of Standards

Mathematics and science standards sought more than a revision of the coverage and sequencing of mathematics topics. As discussed in Chapter 2, they also sought fundamental changes in what counted as mathematical and scientific knowledge and what was involved in doing mathematical and scientific inquiry in schools. School-district policies offered weak and erratic support for these aspects of the reform proposals advanced by standards.

To begin with, standards proposed transforming mathematics and science education to emphasize more intellectually rigorous content; the standards envisioned a K–12 curriculum that achieved a better balance between principled and procedural knowledge. For example, it was not just that the multiplication of decimals should be taught in fifth grade, but that students should also master principled mathematics knowledge (for example, the concept of place value). Topic coverage and sequencing, however, were the extent of support for the standards in two-thirds of the school districts. Policies in these districts focused chiefly on the coverage and sequencing of mathematics and science topics, failing to press any fundamental reconceptualization of mathematics and science knowledge. Support for state and national standards was partial and lukewarm. We found evidence of support for more fundamental changes in content coverage in only a third of the school districts. With respect to mathematics, district policies in suburban Pleasant Valley and Parkwood and in rural Riverville were supportive of these fundamental changes. The situation was similar for science, with the instructional policies in the same two suburban school districts and in rural Littleton supporting a reconceptualizing of what counted as science and mathematics knowledge in ways that resonated with the standards.

State and national standards also sought to transform what students learned about doing mathematics and science in school. They wanted students to understand mathematical and scientific inquiry in ways that were intellectually sophisticated and authentic; doing mathematics should involve more than manipulating numbers to compute right answers, and doing science should entail more than following cookbook recipes to carry out experiments. Again, instructional policies in six of the school districts failed to endorse these complex changes in mathematics and / or science education. For example, instructional policies in these six districts failed to reflect several central themes of the mathematics standards, including mathematics as communication and mathematics as reasoning; these themes were central to state and national reformers' efforts to change what it meant to do mathematics in school. Similarly, while "hands-on science" was a prominent idea in district policies, in these six school districts, science instruction approximated the traditional cookbook laboratory in which students mechanically followed recipes to carry out science experiments, an approach that state standards were trying to get schools to abandon.

Despite considerable effort by district officials, district policies in six districts provided relatively weak or low support for the mathematics and science standards. Only four districts—two suburban districts in both mathematics and science, a rural district in mathematics, and another rural district in science—provided strong or high support for the more complex changes in mathematics and science education advanced by standards. The effect of state standards on district policymaking, though consistent on some matters, thus was weak and inconsistent when it came to the more complex epistemological and instructional changes. While instructional policies in some school districts amplified the state's message about reforming education, instructional policies in most districts drowned out much of this message.

Conclusion

My account offers a glimmer of hope for public policy, especially when contrasted with most implementation scholarship, which is replete with accounts of local agents' and agencies' inattention to state and federal policies. State education policymakers in Michigan were successful in getting school districts to take notice of their proposals for mathematics and science education. Indeed, for a resource-strapped state department of education, it was a blessing that school districts took such notice: absent the active involvement of local school districts, it was difficult to imagine how Michigan's state-level mathematics and science policymakers had any chance of reaching the thousands of Michigan schoolteachers spread across 545 school districts.

Blessings are often mixed. That local school districts in Michigan responded to state standards with a flurry of local policymaking activity might be a blessing for those state policymakers who, on a shoestring budget, sought such fundamental change in science and mathematics education. But the extent of that blessing depended on whether and the extent to which school-district policies supported state policymakers' proposals for reforming science and mathematics education. School-district policies provided strong support for state standards at one level, but at another level they offered mixed and often weak or low support. Only three school districts provided strong support for the ideas pressed by the standards.

Documenting the effects of standards on school-district policymaking is one important component of policy analysis. It is also important to unpack the mechanisms that help account for the uneven progress of standards in school-district policymaking. Figuring out why some school districts developed policies that provided strong support for state and national standards while other districts' policies offered weak support is an important part of the policy analysis task. The magnitude of the differences was tremendous. Unraveling this puzzle is the subject of the next two chapters.

CHAPTER 4

Making Policy, Making Sense

Sonny naughton worked diligently to revise Littleton's policies about mathematics and science education in a direction that he believed supported both state and national standards. For Naughton, developing policies to support the standards involved three things. First, it required specifying and sequencing the mathematics and science topics for each grade level so they were consistent with the standards, especially the state assessment system. Second, how teachers "deliver information" to students had to change. Specifically, Naughton wanted classrooms in which students were engaged in "group activities, cooperative learning activities," "a lot of manipulative use," and "peer coaching" where they were not simply "sitting behind a desk with a calculator." Third, mathematics and science lessons, indeed instruction in general, should "be planned around a thematic approach," to create "an integrated, collaborative math-science curriculum." Naughton elaborated: "There is no reason that what is taught in science cannot be reinforced in mathematics, cannot be reinforced by writing a science report in English . . . let them see the importance of what they're doing and how everything ties together."

While Ann Smith, Lakeside's chief science education policymaker, would agree with some of Naughton's ideas about science education, she would also be unsatisfied. For Smith, the science standards were about two key ideas. The first concerned revising the science content, including transforming the science topics that were covered in the K–12 curriculum. But most important for Smith was putting much more emphasis on scientific "concepts that are fundamental." As she put it, "No matter where you go or what job you're in, some basic concepts about how heat energy works . . . are important." The second idea involved creating a curriculum that developed students' appreciation for scientific inquiry as involving careful observation, constructing knowledge based on these observations and reflecting on that knowledge in light of scientific concepts, and determining the relevance and validity of evidence. In Smith's view, the science standards were pressing a vision of scientific inquiry that went beyond the generic cookbook recipe laboratories that had been a staple of science education since the 1960s.

Linda Burton, rural Riverville's curriculum director, would agree with Sonny Naughton's vision for mathematics education. For Burton, mathematics lessons should involve "a lot of discussion" with "kids working together in groups" and asking questions of each other and of the teacher. But Burton would also have found his ideas about mathematics education wanting. For Burton, the mathematics standards were first and foremost about transforming the sort of mathematics students learned in school. As she put it, "The key is understanding the concept." In her opinion, revising the mathematics content covered in the curriculum involved more than adding topics or changing topic sequencing; it meant ensuring that students had the opportunity to learn and understand important mathematical concepts.

Rhonda Burlington had similar ideas. For Burlington, the standards supported shifting urban Redwood's mathematics program from one that was entirely focused on computation to one that paid attention to both computational and conceptual knowledge. Students "need to know the importance of conceptual knowledge and that conceptual knowledge brings them understanding and involves thinking," Burlington explained. "I think they need to know the place of procedural knowledge and the place of learning algorithms and rules to perform, but that that is not the only important piece of mathematics education. It always has been, but it is not."

Reconstructing Policy Messages

Sonny Naughton, Linda Burton, and other district policymakers heeded the mathematics and science standards. State policy, and in many cases national standards, were very much on their horizons, although for some more prominently than for others. Michigan's efforts to revise mathematics and science education did not fall victim to local inattention, a central antagonist in conventional accounts of implementation failure.

District policymakers were eager to pay attention to the advice that the standards offered about instruction. They certainly groused and grumbled about state policy. But their grousing focused more on the state's constantly changing compliance procedures rather than on the substance of the state's policy. Moreover, such grumbling was far from resistance to the standards. Eagerly revising Littleton's mathematics and science education policies, Sonny Naughton was not trying to sabotage local adoption of the state's mathematics and science standards. On the contrary, like most other district policymakers he was championing the standards. Hence, differences among school districts in their support for the standards cannot be accounted for in terms of district policymakers' unwillingness to take direction from standards.

Limited school-district capacity is another popular antagonist in tales of implementation failure. This explanation assumes that district policymakers understood the instructional changes pressed by the standards but lacked the know-how to develop policies and programs to support these changes. Uneven support for the standards from one school district to the next resulted from differences among districts in terms of their knowledge, skill, and materials to carry out the ideas proposed by standards. As the opening pages of this chapter illuminate, however, the assumption that district policymakers understood the ideas pressed by standards in similar ways or in ways that were consistent with state and national reformers is especially problematic.

Tales of inattention, as well as recalcitrant and change-averse bureaucrats who intentionally or unintentionally sabotage policy proposals, abound in the implementation literature. In trying to account for the uneven progress of state standards in school districts' policymaking initiatives, however, I found conventional explanations unsatisfactory. I develop an explanation in this chapter that centers on the ideas about changing mathematics and science education that district policymakers understood from and about standards.

It was not motivation to change that threatened the local adoption of the standards. As a Littleton school board member explained, "The district administrators want to do good. But they don't know what good is." It was the competing ideas about what it meant to change mathematics and science education that kept the standards' more fundamental ideas from finding their way into school-district policies and classroom practice.

Naughton, Burton, and Burlington were committed to reconstructing their district's policies to support the standards. Indeed, all three understood the standards as entailing change for the mathematics content covered in school. But for Naughton the push to revise content coverage centered on what and when particular mathematics topics were covered. Burton and Burlington understood things differently. For them, the standards entailed much more fundamental changes in content coverage; the standards were a critique of a K–12 curriculum that was top-heavy with mathematical rules, formulas, procedures, and computational skills—procedural mathematical knowledge. They understood the standards to be pressing for a more balanced mathematical curriculum in which students got to learn about key mathematical concepts—principled mathematical knowledge. Not only should students be able to add, subtract, and follow the procedure for multiplying fractions, but they should also understand and be able to explain relations among concepts such as "place value" and "equivalence." Burton and Burlington had fundamentally different understandings of what the standards entailed for mathematical content coverage compared with Naughton.

That Sonny Naughton would see things as he did is not surprising. For Sonny, like most of us, mathematics entails rules and formulas that we memorize and apply, preferably accurately and quickly, to solve algorithms. Occasionally these rules and formulas have very practical applications when we are faced with extraordinary and, as is the case more often, ordinary tasks such as balancing the checkbook or calculating the amount of carpet needed to refurbish the living room. That mathematics would involve anything more is something that escapes most of us. And for those who do recognize that mathematics involves principled knowledge, they are frequently content to leave such erudite matters to mathematicians. Understanding mathematics as procedural knowledge, it was difficult for Sonny Naughton to grasp that the standards encouraged a mathematics curriculum that balanced principled and procedural knowledge.

Sonny Naughton was eager to revise Littleton's policies to support the mathematics standards. But in order to aspire to develop policies that supported a curriculum that balanced procedural and principled mathematical knowledge, Naughton would have

to first understand that mathematics involved more than procedures, rules, and computational skills. All the will in the world
could not have made things otherwise. After all, it is difficult to
want to do something that one cannot comprehend in the first
place.

Making Sense of Policy

Sense-making is not a simple decoding process of a given stimuli.
Psychologists portray it as an active process of interpretation that
draws on the sense-maker's experiences, knowledge, beliefs, and
attitudes (Carey, 1985; Schank and Abelson, 1977; von Glasersfeld, 1989). Knowledge and experiences are integrated into a web
of interdependent relationships—what psychologists refer to as
scripts or schemas. We filter new incoming information through
these scripts (Rumelhart, 1980). The sense we make thus depends
on the sense we already have; our existing knowledge is a primary resource in the development of new, sometimes better, understandings. Hence, a policy's messages about changing behavior are not inert ideas that reside in the legislation or policy
regulations and that are transmitted unaltered into district
policymakers' minds.

Sense-making involves multiple processes (Weick, 1995).
Sense-makers notice some things in their environment while at
the same time ignoring many others. Watching the same movie
or reading the same book, two individuals are often drawn to different events or incidents. Having noticed an event, sense-makers
frame it and connect it to their prior experiences and knowledge
(Mandler, 1984). The new is always noticed, framed, and understood in light of what is already known.

Familiarity Breeds Attention

With a limited capacity for attention, most of us ignore a great
deal of our environment. Attending to everything would be im-

possible, if we ever wanted to get anything done. We develop through life lenses that filter what gets our attention. Familiarity is one such filter; we are drawn to those things that are familiar to us based on our prior experiences, and we tend to ignore ideas that do not fit with our existing scripts.

Accordingly, ideas about reforming mathematics and science education that were more familiar to district policymakers got their attention, while the more novel ideas tended to go unnoticed. By the late 1980s, "problem solving," "hands-on activities," and "integration" were popular prescriptions for instructional improvement in education circles. These ideas had been aired and circulating for a couple of decades among practitioners and school reformers. They figured prominently in district policymakers' understandings of the standards. "Hands-on science" and "integration" were the two most prevalent ideas in district policymakers' understandings of the science standards. Eighty-three percent of the forty-six district policymakers involved in making science education policy spoke about "hands-on" science and over 54 percent discussed integration. Indeed, these two ideas were articulated by at least one policymaker in each school district. With respect to the mathematics standards, "hands-on" mathematics or using manipulatives was the most prominent idea, referred to by 45 percent of the eighty district policymakers involved with making policy about mathematics education. More than a third of the sample, over 38 percent, mentioned problem solving in mathematics. It was the only theme from the four central organizing themes of the mathematics standards that figured prominently in district policymakers' understandings.

Less familiar ideas did not fare as well with district policymakers. With respect to the science standards, "constructivist learning" and "conceptual understanding" were not nearly as prominent in district policymakers' understandings. Whereas 45 percent of the forty-six district science policymakers referenced conceptual understanding, only 13 percent mentioned "constructivist learning." In three districts, constructivist learning was mentioned by none of the science education policymakers. District policymakers mentioned hands-on six times more often than constructivist learning. In only two districts was conceptual understanding discussed by more than half of the district policymakers responsible for science education. The more novel reform ideas encouraged by the mathematics standards met a similar fate. Only 20 percent of the eighty district policymakers mentioned mathematics as communication, and only 17.5 percent mentioned mathematics as reasoning, understanding, or both.

Conserving Existing Understandings

We are told that old habits die hard. Mental scripts are equally resilient. When faced with new knowledge or experiences, we work to *assimilate* them into their existing knowledge scripts, or we adjust our scripts to *accommodate* the new knowledge (Piaget, 1972). Assimilation is a conserving process striving to "make the unfamiliar familiar, to reduce the new to the old" (Flavell, 1963, p. 50). But the development of new understanding requires that existing scripts be overhauled to accommodate new knowledge.

Regrettably for social reformers and others who seek to foster fundamental changes in people's knowledge, assimilation has the under hand (Confrey, 1990). Sense-making tends to be a conserving process. Accessing what is known and familiar to make sense out of new knowledge, we tend to preserve our existing mental scripts rather than radically overhaul them. This happens for at least two reasons. First, new ideas are understood as familiar friends—ideas that are already known to us. Second, we rely on surface or superficial similarities between new knowledge about something and our existing scripts for that something. When we access ideas in our memory related to some new knowledge, we tend to draw analogs to surface features rather than to the structural features, even when these deeper structural features might be crucial for developing new understandings (Gentner, 1989; Gentner and Landers, 1985; Gentner, Rattermann, and Forbus, 1994).

Misunderstanding the New as the Old. District policymakers often overinterpreted reform ideas as similar to some of their existing ideas. Influenced by expectations from their existing scripts, they perceived ideas about reforming mathematics and science education as more familiar than they were. Some district policymakers understood mathematical problem-solving as identical to the story problems that had been a staple in mathematics textbooks for years. One district policymaker explained confidently, "It's not any different. Story problems and word problems, they're the same, been around for years." A policymaker in a rural district candidly acknowledged that she could not see what was new about mathematical problem solving. "I'm not clear myself what's new about problem solving . . . I mean, is this different from the word story problems that I got when I was a kid?" The situation was similar with respect to district policymakers' understanding of the science standards.

Even when district policymakers appreciated that ideas such as problem solving entailed some new understanding and change, they still perceived them as similar to some existing ideas. For many district policymakers, problem solving was all about linking school mathematics more directly to real-life situations. Problem solving involved engaging students with realistic story problems and problem situations that were connected to real-life situations:

If you read mathematics problems, they are put in a real meaningful context . . . Things like percentages in sixth grade have something to do with giving a sale with so much percentage off and so on. The students will be able to figure out if they've saved money or whatever, and how much money they've saved.

I think problem solving is more realistic . . . It's math as solving something that they might encounter. If I go to the store and spend so much money, how much am I going to get back, you know, the type of thing that's real-world to the kids. I think it's important to make a mathematics problem more realistic.

District policymakers understood the standards in terms of making the mathematics students work on problems more relevant to their everyday lives.

Problem solving as a reform idea did entail change for these district policymakers. And their understanding of problem solving was certainly not contrary to the standards. But by connecting problem solving to an already familiar idea—making the mathematics curriculum more relevant to students' lives—they missed key aspects of mathematical problem solving as developed in the standards. As discussed in Chapter 2, problem solving, as encouraged by the standards, involved more than making mathematical problems more interesting and relevant; it entailed making mathematics problematic in order that students would explore further and consider alternative conjectures (NCTM, 1989, 1991). Problem solving, according to the standards, should serve as a context for learning both principled and procedural knowledge. But by interpreting problem solving on the basis of their existing scripts for mathematics and mathematics instruction, these district policymakers understood the idea chiefly in terms of changing the activities for teaching procedural mathematical knowledge. Even when pressed, these district policymakers said nothing to suggest that problem solving might involve placing greater emphasis on principled mathematical knowledge. A district policymaker summed up the situation, noting, "You gonna still add 'em up, you're gonna still do the division, don't spend all your time on isolated addition, subtraction, multiplication, division facts. Make it meaningful, you know, give it some real-life importance." District policymakers' understandings of problem solving involved tweaking rather than overhauling their existing scripts. Having assimilated new knowledge about mathematics education into their existing scripts, these district policymakers' shifted the thrust of the standards from an attempt to balance principled and procedural mathematical knowledge to one in which new story problems were the primary change message.

Noticing Surface Rather Than Structural Similarities. Surface features are effective memory triggers when making connections between some new information and one's existing mental script. For district policymakers accessing and applying their knowledge scripts to make sense of standards, surface features were especially salient. Most district policymakers focused on surface features of the ideas pressed by standards; the mathematics and science standards were about changing student grouping arrangements, making the instructional activities that students worked on more relevant to their lives, revising instructional strategies, adding more laboratories and experiments to science lessons, and including new forms of the story problem, among other things. In focusing on the more concrete surface-level aspects of the reform ideas, they tended to miss the deeper structural or conceptual changes in doing science and mathematics as urged by the standards. Most district policymakers understood the reform ideas in ways that preserved conventional views of mathematics and science as procedural knowledge, teaching as telling or showing, and learning as remembering.

Consider for example scientific activity, a core reform idea in the standards. Most district policymakers understood the standards' push for attention to scientific activity in terms of "hands-on science." For some district policymakers, hands-on science in-volved introducing activities that went beyond the conventional textbook and lecture-dominated approach to teaching science:

> Kids learn by doing, not by listening or by reading. You learn by doing and that's what kids are doing now.

> The idea is to have more hands-on, let the kids manipulate stuff and measure stuff, you know, physically, and push a rod or do a pulley or stuff like that. It used to be that any kind of sci-ence that was done, even back when I first started, was open to page ten and do the first five problems and we'll discuss them—and the teacher can draw a pulley on the board and show a rope.

These district policymakers' perception of scientific activity cen-tered on more concrete, surface-level aspects of the activity—learning by doing, having students manipulate materials, getting students more active. But as Chapter 2 made clear, state standards treated scientific "activity" as involving a fundamental change in scientific inquiry. It was about encouraging students to seek out questions and problems, develop viable solutions, and defend and justify their ideas. Most district policymakers' understandings re-flected none of these deeper conceptual ideas. Instead, they un-derstood the science standards in terms of new instructional ap-proaches that preserved the conventional cookbook experiments and staged activities.

Other district policymakers' understandings of hands-on sci-ence centered on a means of engaging students with different "learning styles." These district policymakers understood experi-ments and science laboratory work as essential in creating an en-vironment in which all students, regardless of learning style, were able to learn:

People learn differently and different sensory modalities are different for people. It also adds fun and interest to what you are doing if you are doing something instead of just reading about it or listening about it.

I think the hands-on approach is important . . . I think the more senses that we involve in the learning process, the more likely we are to learn and the more people you're likely to touch because some of us learn in different ways. The more varied our approach is to teaching—it's like a shotgun—the more likely we are to hit students.

For these district policymakers, hands-on science represented transforming instructional activities to involve students' different learning styles. It did not, however, involve any reconceptualization of science content or scientific inquiry.

Still other district policymakers' understandings of hands-on science concentrated on motivating students to learn by making science education more interesting:

Students are active . . . Just give kids a bunch of batteries and wires and light bulbs and they get turned on.

My own philosophy is that if students have a chance to use things, to touch them, to put them together, to take them apart, whatever, they remember what they're doing.

For these district policymakers, hands-on was understood as a means to spur interest in science. Motivating students to learn is undeniably important. Still, although these local understandings did entail change for science instruction, they were firmly grounded in the more concrete surface features of the ideas about scientific inquiry pressed by the standards. Science learning was still mostly about remembering, and science teaching about showing and telling.

Reconstructed Reform Ideas. In district policymakers' sense-making from and about standards, assimilation trumped accommodation. Using their existing scripts to make sense of ideas about reforming mathematics and science, most district policymakers tended to patch their existing scripts for mathematics, science, and instruction rather than overhaul them. Most noticed familiar ideas, such as group work, using manipulatives, and real-life story problems; but lacking a mental framework to connect and explain the more unfamiliar ideas, they devoted less attention to them and often overlooked them entirely.

Nearly 80 percent of the district policymakers involved with making policy about mathematics constructed understandings that preserved conventional views of mathematics as procedural knowledge and doing mathematics as mostly computing right answers. Their understandings focused on surface-level features of the reform ideas such as using manipulatives, new grouping arrangements, and more real-life mathematics story problems. The deeper structural changes pressed by standards did not figure in these district policymakers' understandings. Most district policymakers also constructed surface-level understandings of the science standards. For example, more than 75 percent of district policymakers constructed surface-level understandings of hands-on science, missing the deeper, more conceptual elements of scientific activity.

Constructing Deeper-Level Understandings

Major restructuring of existing knowledge scripts is difficult, but it does happen. Our understandings do change. Cognitive scientists have shown that a major restructuring of mental scripts is extremely difficult but possible through sustained grappling with new ideas (Strike and Posner, 1985; Carey, 1985). Further, expertise in an area facilitates the development of new deeper-level understandings in that area because experts are less likely to be distracted by superficial similarities. Instead, experts tend to hone in on the deeper structural similarities between their existing scripts and new information, those aspects of an idea that are more significant conceptually (Chase and Simon, 1974; Chi, Feltovich, and Glaser, 1981).

Some district policymakers did construct understandings from and about standards that involved more fundamental changes in their thinking about mathematics and science in school. For almost a quarter (24 percent) of the forty-six district policymakers who discussed hands-on science, their understandings focused on deeper conceptual changes in science education. For these district policymakers, the standards involved fundamentally changing the science content that students were exposed to, what it meant to do scientific inquiry, and in some cases what it meant to teach and learn science. They understood the standards as being about giving more attention to principled knowledge in science and enabling students to develop more sophisticated understandings of scientific inquiry. Similarly, just over 20 percent (seventeen) of district policymakers constructed understandings of the mathematics standards that involved deeper, more fundamental changes in what counted as mathematical knowledge and doing mathematics in school.

Consider Ann Smith, who was the driving force for revising rural Lakeside's policies about science education. A physical education teacher with a minor in biology, Smith had devoted considerable time over the past five years to developing her expertise in science and science education. Moreover, Smith spent substantial time and effort, inside and outside the Littleton school district, figuring out how to improve science education. For Smith, the push for improvement in classroom scientific activity involved a fundamental transformation of what students experienced as scientific inquiry in schools. She was openly critical of those who equated the standards' press for scientific inquiry with simply doing more hands-on activities or more cookbook experiments. She argued:

> Hands-on is one of those clichés. And at first, it's just through a bunch of activities. But to me, it's not doing activities that is absolutely essential, but it's the web that connects the activities and the building on and discussion and reflections that you do with the class afterward. So, to me, the activity itself gets the kids interested in the book and wanting to come back, and then it's the skill of the teachers to weave those together and to incorporate the science knowledge in the activity.

For Smith, hands-on science was about developing scientific habits of mind in students—encouraging them to see connections among scientific ideas and pushing them to construct and justify their own ideas. She elaborated, "We stress the scientific method throughout everything so that careful observations are emphasized, not just jumping to conclusions but having some evidence to support them . . . I would go around challenging them after a lab: 'Why do you say this?' 'What's your evidence to back up your conclusion?'" Ann Smith understood scientific activity as involving students in using scientific knowledge to explain and predict the scientific phenomena, to develop questions about these phenomena, and to construct knowledge by reflecting on the findings from the experiments they had designed.

Other district policymakers, albeit a minority, constructed similar understandings of scientific activity.

> They have to draw real conclusions from those experiments. They are going to have to be comfortable with doing stuff or saying, "Well this didn't work," instead of the teacher saying what to do. [They need to be able to ask,] "I wonder what this means?" "What do I need to know in order to do this?"

In science we want them to be more curious and questioning and discovering. It's not just knowledge, it's not just skills, there's also kind of an attitude or a disposition.

For Ann Smith and these other district policymakers, engaging students with the scientific process was more than a motivational ploy. It was more than a way of improving student retention of scientific facts. For these district policymakers, doing science involved more than being able to recite the steps in the scientific process or follow accurately the recipe for a science experiment. It was a way to allow students to engage in scientific inquiry and develop scientific habits. One message that these district policymakers took from the standards was that students needed to appreciate that scientific investigations were not just isolated activities that always produced some anticipated or predetermined conclusion. Hands-on denoted fundamental change in what it meant to do scientific inquiry in classrooms; it involved defending and justifying one's findings when questioned, cultivating in students scientific habits of mind and dispositions, and making the connections between scientific investigations and scientific theory more explicit.

Undoubtedly some of these district policymakers had more sophisticated understandings of mathematics and science education in advance of the standards. Still, most reported that their understandings of mathematics had evolved tremendously in the few years prior to the study.

Local Understanding and District Policy Support for Standards

District policymakers' understandings were important in accounting for the extent to which the policies they developed supported the standards. In school districts where policies provided strong support for standards (high-support districts), more district policymakers had developed deeper-level understandings of the reform ideas. In contrast, in low-support districts, most district policymakers expressed surface-level understandings of the reform ideas, which suggested that they had assimilated the reform ideas into their existing scripts for mathematics and science education.

With respect to mathematics, almost 95 percent of the district policymakers in the six low-support school districts expressed surface-level understandings. In contrast, in high-support school districts, district policymakers' understandings were evenly split between surface-level and deeper-level understandings.* Policymakers in the high implementation districts were more likely to have constructed deeper-level understandings of the mathematics reforms.

The situation was similar with respect to the science standards. As discussed in Chapter 3, only three of the nine school districts were developing policies that approximated the more fundamental changes in science content and science inquiry pressed by the standards. More than 55 percent of the district policymakers who constructed deeper level understandings worked in one of these three high-support school districts. Three out of four policymakers in the six school districts that provided low support for the science standards had surface-level understandings of hands-on science. District policymakers in low implementation districts were three times more likely to have surface-level rather than deeper-level understandings of the reform ideas. Although we cannot infer a causal relation between district policymakers' understandings and the level of support for standards in their districts, the evidence suggests a relationship between the two variables. Moreover, these patterns cut across the formal positions and job responsibilities of district policymakers. Those who de-

---

* A chi-square test for independence revealed a significant relationship between district leaders' type of understanding and the level of implementation in his or her district ($\chi^2 = 20.82 > 7.88$; df $= 1$, n $= 82$, $\alpha = .05$).

veloped district policies and programs for mathematics education had a variety of positions. Some were district-office administrators or subject area specialists. Others were school principals. Still others were regular classroom teachers. District policymakers who worked at the school or classroom level were just as likely to construct surface-level understandings as those who worked in the district office. I found no relationship between district leaders' level of understanding and whether their primary position was based in the district office, school, or classroom.

Conclusion

Familiarity was a mixed blessing when it came to district policymakers' sense-making. On the positive side, familiar ideas about reforming instruction got district policymakers' attention. In this way, familiarity contributed to the development of district policies that offered some support for the mathematics and science standards. But there was a negative side: district policymakers understood these familiar ideas through the mental scripts they already had for them.

Processing new knowledge about teaching and learning was a conserving process for district policymakers. Sense-making tends to preserve existing frames rather than radically alter them. New ideas about mathematics and science education either were understood as familiar ones, without sufficient attention to aspects that diverged from the familiar, or were integrated without the restructuring of existing scripts. Most district policymakers developed understandings that just scratched the surface of the ideas pressed by standards, missing deeper, more conceptual core elements such as transforming what counted as knowledge and inquiry in mathematics and science education. The result was only modest change in existing local understanding and thereby in the ideas about mathematics and science education promoted by school-district policies.

A related puzzle concerns why some district policymakers developed deeper-level understandings that resonated more closely with the spirit of the standards, while others constructed surface-level understandings. How was it that Ann Smith or Linda Burton developed deeper understandings of the ideas pressed by the mathematics standards compared with Sonny Naughton? Cognitive theory, as discussed briefly earlier, offers at least two leads—the district policymaker's level of expertise and the opportunities that district policymakers had to grapple with the ideas.

CHAPTER 5

Resources for Sense-Making

LIKE MANY CURRICULUM DIRECTORS in small school districts, Sonny Naughton was a generalist. Mathematics and science education were not his forte. Naughton was successful in writing grants, organizing and managing groups, administrating grants and programs, and mobilizing reform efforts with and beyond the school system. He was satisfied with his surface-level understanding of the mathematics and science standards. He had no reason to suspect that anything was amiss. There was nothing in the weeklong workshop organized by a mathematics textbook publisher or in his reading of the standards that gave him cause for concern. Indeed, by his own account, Naughton's efforts to make sense of the standards were relatively effortless and uncomplicated. He had no need to grapple with reform ideas and no cause to enlist the help of others. Although Naughton interacted with others, went to workshops, and read state and national standards documents, he made sense of the standards mostly on his own, never seeking out opportunities to check his understanding against the interpretations of others. In Naughton's case, making sense of the standards was something of a solo performance, with lots of reform document props but with others backstage.

Circumstances were different for Ann Smith in Lakeside. Smith, who had majored in college in physical education, acquired considerable expertise in science and science education in the early 1990s. She saw herself as a learner who devoted much of her after-school and weekend time to learning about science education. Such an investment of time was necessary because, as Smith tells it, she was a "traditional" science teacher who focused on "covering ground," on the "kind of learning that dealt with memorization." Dissatisfied with her science teaching, which she noted "was really pretty bad," she began to change things. She took courses at the Mathematics and Science Center affiliated with a neighboring university, participated in local and regional committees designed to improve science education, and networked with science educators around the state. According to Smith, these experiences contributed to her learning about science and science education as well as to considerable change in her teaching. As she put it, "I've come through many years of gradual change." Along with developing her expertise in science education and an extensive network of science educators beyond the Lakeview school district, Smith took time to figure out the standards and appreciate their deeper conceptual significance for science education.

Things were also different in Riverville. Linda Burton, Riverville's director of curriculum, was a generalist like Sonny Naughton with limited expertise in mathematics. In Riverville, however, efforts to make sense of the mathematics standards were a collective endeavor. Burton worked closely with Lisa Carter and other lead teachers. Carter, a middle-school mathematics teacher, had considerable expertise in mathematics and extensive classroom experience. Further, as a Ph.D. student at a neighboring university, Carter was continuing to develop her expertise in mathematics education, especially new research on mathematics teaching. Carter, Burton, and their colleagues described their efforts to figure out the mathematics standards as a shared enterprise in which they struggled together to make sense of what the standards might entail for classrooms. They even enlisted the support of mathematics educators at a neighboring university for these efforts. These ongoing deliberations among Riverville's mathematics policymakers and with outside experts took a long time and considerable effort.

Policymaking is resource intensive. It takes time, brain work, and political skill, among other things. Sense-making can also consume a great deal of resources. Though it is frequently portrayed as an effortless process, that is not always the case. Psychologists tell us that the restructuring of our existing knowledge scripts, which is necessary for fundamental change in the way we understand, is difficult (Strike and Posner, 1985). Recall the last time you encountered and recognized some novel idea on a familiar topic. Making a quick note of the time, mental effort, advice from experts, and other resources you used in figuring out the significance of these ideas in order to develop a new way of thinking will give you a sense of the resource dependency of human sense-making. For district policymakers, who understood mathematics and science chiefly in terms of procedural knowledge, developing deeper-level understandings of the ideas pushed by standards would be arduous work.

The Distribution and Deployment of Resources

Sense-making depends on the resources at the sense-makers' disposal. This is as true for district policymakers trying to figure out scientific inquiry as it is for fourth-graders grappling with fractions for the first time. Three categories of resources were pivotal in district policymakers' sense-making from and about standards. The substance and packaging of the new information aside for now, many of these resources concern sense-makers and their circumstances. Individual knowledge, expertise, and experience can be thought of as human resources. Expertise enables sense-making, whereas its lack constrains the process. Psychologists remind us that social resources are also critical in sense-making. Social networks often serve as sources of information and sometimes work as sounding boards for the sense one makes. Social trust and a sense of mutual obligation can support sense-making. These social resources, when present, can enable sense-making and, when absent, can limit it. Time and materials that typically have price tags are also critical for sense-making. These resources were unevenly distributed and deployed among district policymakers and school districts.

The distribution of resources was one matter. The recognition and deployment of resources for sense-making was another. Resources often lie dormant and go unused. Moreover, resources can be used for an array of projects, and their deployment can be more or less efficient. Hence, it is not just the distribution of resources that matters when it comes to district policymakers' sense-making. Even human resources can go unused or underused, as echoed in the popular remark, "What a waste of a great mind." Both the distribution and activation of a school district's resources for making sense are important considerations.

Sense-Making and Human Resources

District policymakers' knowledge and experience were critical resources in their sense-making. Knowledge, expertise, and skill can be thought of in terms of human capital in that they can enable sense-making from and about the standards. Human capital is acquired through the development of skills and capabilities that enable people to perform in new ways (Schultz, 1961; Becker, 1964). District policymakers who were knowledgeable about mathematics and science education did not lose the forest for the trees; they focused on the deeper, more conceptual features of the reform ideas rather than their surface features.

Some were subject matter experts. Others had developed or were acquiring expertise in teaching and learning. Ann Smith, who spearheaded rural Lakeside's policymaking about science education, although not a science major herself, had returned to school to pursue a master's degree in science and science education. The science coordinator in suburban Pleasant Valley had spent many years working as an industrial scientist. Becoming a science educator later in her career, she learned about science instruction through involvement with some state and national science education agencies and by spending time observing science classrooms. Riverville's Lisa Carter had considerable expertise in mathematics and developed her knowledge of mathematics education through connections with a local university. These women had sophisticated understandings of science, mathematics, and science education in these two domains. Further, they were continuing to expand their knowledge and skills through connections outside their districts, ongoing work with colleagues, and teaching in their districts.

Human Resources and the Will to Understand. District policymakers' will to learn depended in part on their knowledge. With limited expertise in mathematics and science, Sonny Naughton was not aware that his understandings of the standards were underdeveloped; he perceived no need to develop his understanding. In contrast, Lisa Carter's expertise in mathematics and mathematics education was such that she appreciated the need to learn more in order to understand the ideas urged by the standards. To want to know more about something, it is necessary to have some threshold-level expertise in order to appreciate the need to learn.

In high-support school districts, district policymakers were disposed to learning about mathematics and science instruction. These district policymakers understood that if they were going to change instruction in their districts, they would have to learn, and they saw this learning as ongoing. For some, such as Ann Smith, this involved acquiring both subject-matter knowledge and pedagogical knowledge. For others, learning centered on science or mathematics pedagogy. Suburban Pleasant Valley's science coordinator, for example, spent considerable time learning about science instruction. She explained, "When I need to know something, I find it, I read it, look it up, talk to people about it." District policymakers' motivation to comprehend and learn depended in part on whether their existing knowledge enabled them to appreciate their need to learn.

The will to understand and change depends on realizing that current understanding and practice are somehow inadequate. To want to do much of what the standards proposed, let alone to carry out these proposals, district policymakers would need to understand mathematics and science in ways that differed substantially from their existing understandings. It is difficult to desire to do something that one cannot comprehend.

The Limits of Human Resources. District policymakers' expertise was crucial in supporting the sort of sense-making that was necessary in developing deeper-level understanding of the standards. Each of the nine districts had at least one or two individuals who were knowledgeable about mathematics and science education, albeit some more than others. Still, most school districts failed to develop policies that provided strong support for the ideas advanced by the standards.

While individual expertise was necessary, it was not sufficient. What was critical was whether district policymakers recognized, understood the importance of, and mobilized these human resources. Riverville's Linda Burton explained: "Significant change happens when you get beyond the key leaders. The key leaders will always have the good ideas, and they'll implement them in their classrooms. You need to take advantage of these key leaders and offer others opportunities to learn from them." With respect to human resources, mobilizing the human resources available in the school district to develop the knowledge of others was critical in developing deeper-level understandings of the ideas pressed by standards.

In high-support school districts, the leadership managed not only to invest in the human resources of a handful of knowledgeable individuals, but also to marshal and deploy these individuals in developing a knowledgeable collective. For example, in rural Riverville, district administrators identified and capitalized on teacher leaders like Lisa Carter who were knowledgeable and committed to learning more about the mathematics standards. They invested in these teachers' learning and supported their efforts to help other teachers and administrators in the district develop deep understandings of the mathematics standards. In high-support districts, individual experts were recognized and deployed in the development of a critical mass of individuals with deeper-level understandings of the ideas pressed by the standards.

The situation was different in low-support school districts such as rural Littleton. Mathematics was not Sonny Naughton's area of expertise. But Littleton did have expertise in mathematics education. For example, Lisa Yarrow, a middle-school mathematics teacher, had a sophisticated understanding of mathematics instruction. A latecomer to teaching, she had developed an appreciation for mathematical concepts and the importance of teaching them to students as part of her teacher preparation program, which included a minor in mathematics. Sonny Naughton and his colleagues, however, never tapped Yarrow's expertise in their efforts to make sense of the mathematics standards. Yarrow reported that when she talked with colleagues in Littleton about her understanding of the mathematics standards, she was met with silence. Yarrow noted that she had given up trying to influence her colleagues' understandings of the standards. She said, "I just don't say anything at meetings anymore. I stop trying to push my ideas on anyone." In Littleton, district policymakers did not capitalize on valuable expertise to support their efforts to make sense of the mathematics standards.

Social Resources

Sense-making is seldom accomplished singlehandedly. It is not the solitary enterprise that we often make it out to be. Social resources are part of the circumstances in which sense-making takes place and refer to social networks as well as the relations among individuals in a group. Often termed social capital by sociologists and economists, social relations can enable the production of both economic and noneconomic goods (Bourdieu, 1986; Coleman, 1988; Portes, 1998). "Social capital inheres in the structure of relations between actors and among actors," notes James Coleman (1988, p. 98). Social resources such as network ties, both within and beyond an organization, can facilitate the transfer and development of knowledge. Developing social capital involves changing the way people relate with each other in order to facilitate the attainment of goals that would not be possible without these relations.

Social resources for sense-making were substantially different in high-support districts compared with low-support districts. Specifically, two forms of social resources—social networks, and norms of trust and a sense of obligation among individuals—were more prevalent in high-support districts.

District policymakers' links to sources of knowledge within and beyond the local school system were important in facilitating their sense-making from and about the mathematics and science standards. Formal and informal professional networks were important social resources, facilitating the development of district policymakers' knowledge and expertise—that is, the districts' human resources. In the high-support school districts, district policymakers invariably had forged ties to outside agencies or associations that were working to reform mathematics or science education. They actively participated with these external agencies, using them to gain perspectives on and knowledge about reforming instruction.

For some district policymakers, this meant increased knowledge of the disciplines themselves. For others, it involved understanding mathematics and science teaching and ways to help teachers change their instructional practice. The science coordinator in suburban Pleasant Valley, for example, referred to crucial connections with organizations such as the National Science Resources Board and a National Science Foundation curriculum project. She reported that these connections enabled her to develop the knowledge she needed to set about reforming her district's policies about science education. "They gave me access to a lot of research," she remarked, "and I relate to that." These networks also enabled this district official to gain practical knowledge about implementing new approaches to science education in real classrooms. Through her connections, she visited another school district to observe its attempts to reform science education in practice. What she saw there became an integral part of the program that she eventually created in suburban Pleasant Valley. It also allowed her to anticipate some of the implementation challenges she would face as she worked to fundamentally transform the district's science program. She remarked, "In Virginia, where they've had this science program, I got a chance to talk with people at all levels . . . it gave me a snapshot of what I've learned since then, down the road, where the problems would be." These connections also helped convince her that it was possible to completely revise science instruction in her district.

Rich with social resources, high-support school districts accessed a variety of professional networks and contacts to learn about mathematics and science. Riverville's Linda Burton explained that a variety of sources, including university professors, professional journals, associations, and research, were much more influential than state policy in Riverville's policymaking about mathematics education. She remarked, "We talk about the research, we talk about journal articles, we talk about the NCTM standards . . . We use that as sort of a professional development."

Similarly, Lakeside's Ann Smith had forged ties to a variety of regional and state-level organizations concerned with reforming science education.

Social networks were especially important in smaller districts, where financial and staffing resources were not always abundant. As an administrator in rural Riverville explained: "With a small district like this, we really had very little money for curriculum development and, more importantly, very little time and money to think about what is correct in that direction. People that have the expertise are at the university . . . so that's the direction we pushed our people." Teacher leaders in Riverville established ties with a neighboring university; over time, these connections helped them develop deeper understandings of the mathematics standards and provided them with an accessible source of expertise when problems arose. Networks enabled the district to invest in building knowledge and expertise (human resources) for fundamental change in mathematics education.

Networks also enabled high-support districts to develop knowledge tailored to the particular challenges they were encountering in reforming instruction. The usability of knowledge depends in part on the situation in which it is acquired. If learning is to affect behavior, it must not only change knowledge and beliefs, but also occur in or be linked to the contexts in which the learning is to be used (Brown, Collins, and Duguid, 1989; Resnick, 1988). Some networks, especially those that established strong ties between district policymakers and external experts over time, facilitated the development of knowledge that was closely linked to or situated in district policymakers' attempts to figure out the standards and their entailments for mathematics and science education. Only two school districts had forged these sorts of networks.

Rural Riverville's association with a neighboring university is illustrative. By interacting with two faculty members at this university, Riverville's teacher leaders had developed knowledge and skills about mathematics education that were usable and robust because the learning was situated in their ongoing attempts to develop district policies that supported the mathematics standards. One faculty member, for example, piloted a middle-school mathematics curriculum in Riverville. The pilot project allowed local educators to talk with an outside expert about revising mathematics education. Another faculty member worked with Lisa Carter, the middle-school teacher who led Riverville's mathematics reforms, in her classroom over a ten-week period as she implemented a new mathematics curriculum. Carter reported that the experience encouraged her to rethink her practice; she "started to understand the complexity of this new teaching much more." Moreover, the experience helped her to figure out ways of helping other teachers in the district to rethink changing their mathematics instruction.

Trust among district administrators and teachers was a second social resource. Those districts that had made the greatest strides in revising their mathematics and science policies in ways that resonated with standards were also ones with a sense of trust among educators within the district. Trust was essential for genuine collaboration among district policymakers, enabling them to work together to develop a shared understanding of the standards. Trust facilitated conversations about instruction and its improvement among district policymakers—conversations that provided a venue for local experts to share their understandings. Further, group interactions can aid sense-making because they bring to the surface insights and perspectives that otherwise might not be made visible to the group (Brown and Campione, 1990; Brown, Collins, and Duguid, 1989). While interacting with each other, individuals can explicate tacit beliefs as they are prompted to summarize and articulate their interpretations. As arguments become more explicit, inconsistencies in one's argument tend to be highlighted, revealing flaws that were not apparent before. Social trust created an environment in which local educators were comfortable discussing their understandings of and reservations about the ideas they understood from and about the standards. Such conversations were essential for the development of deeper conceptual understandings of the reform ideas.

The importance of social trust in district policymakers' sensemaking is illuminated when we consider three school districts of similar size—Riverville, Pleasant Grove, and Littleton. While Riverville's policies offered high support for the mathematics standards, Pleasant Grove's and Littleton's policies offered low support.

There was a strong sense of trust among district policymakers in Riverville, a trust that enabled them to collaborate on figuring out the mathematics standards. Administrators and teachers worked together over a number of years to develop a shared understanding of the mathematics standards, crafting policies and intervention strategies to implement this shared understanding districtwide. A teacher explained that the "administration is very open to people trying things, gives them credit for what they do, and makes it very positive that way." The superintendent explained: "You have to allow teachers to do instructional reform." He elaborated, noting that an administrative approach that facilitated teachers as leaders of instructional reform and provided them with the space and time to work together was critical in nurturing real instructional change. Because they trusted each other, educators were willing to talk with one another about their understandings of the mathematic standards and promote each others' understandings.

Circumstances were different in urban Pleasant Grove. Some district policymakers in Pleasant Grove were knowledgeable about mathematics and networked with individuals and agencies involved with the mathematics standards. Social trust, however, was in short supply in Pleasant Grove. District administrators had assigned time for collaborative work on the mathematics standards, but relations between teachers and administrators were tense. Administrators spoke openly about teacher resistance as the major hurdle in reforming instruction. A school principal said, "If I were to leave instructional change to the teachers, it would never happen. It will have to be integrated into our curriculum and it has to be sanctioned by the board, which will say 'This is what we want.' Other than that we won't get it." Teachers described the district administration as unsupportive. A teacher remarked, "I don't think most of the teachers here believe they have the administrative leadership that they believe needs to go with that kind of instructional change." Similar tensions were evident among teachers. Pleasant Grove's administrators and teachers never mentioned engaging with their colleagues in discussions about the standards and their entailments for instruction. Such discussions would be difficult considering the lack of trust among them.

Trust, then, was a requisite for the sort of genuine conversations about instruction that enabled district policymakers to grapple with the meaning of the standards. These collaborations allowed more knowledgeable local educators to contribute to the understanding of others, helping to muster the development of a knowledgeable cadre. In turn, this cadre expanded the larger group's overall knowledge about mathematics and science education.

In district policymakers' sense-making, human and social resources worked in tandem. Social resources were instrumental in the sense-making process. But the extent to which social resources were pivotal depended in part on the knowledge of district policymakers—human resources. Such knowledge was necessary for identifying and mobilizing external networks and internal norms of trust in the cause of understanding the standards. For example, the mere existence of internal networks was insufficient to support the sense-making necessary for a deeper understanding of the standards. The potency of social networks depended on how district policymakers used them; they depended on the school district's human resources. Low-support school districts were connected to networks, but there was little evidence of any effort to mobilize these connections in the cause of developing district policymakers' understanding of the standards. As many district policymakers admitted, connections were shallow and ephemeral. In contrast, in high-support school districts networks provided connections to outside resources that district policymakers used to further their understandings of the standards. In these instances, social networks served not only as information channels; they also facilitated district policymakers' sense-making by allowing them to engage in ongoing deliberations about the standards.

Similarly, human resources contributed to the district's sense-making from and about standards, but the extent to which they did depended on school district's social resources. Absent social resources such as trust, deeper conceptual understandings of the standards rarely got beyond one or two district policymakers.

Staffing, Time, and Materials

Most district policymakers, like the rest of us, did not figure out the standards in one sitting. This is to be expected. Sustained engagement with an idea is critical for deep conceptual change. For those district policymakers who developed a deep understanding of the standards, sense-making took considerable time; years rather than months. This is what happened for Burton, Carter, and their colleagues in Riverville. Of course, the availability of time for sense-making depended in part on district staffing. Moreover, materials of various sorts played an important role in district policymakers' sense-making.

Time and staffing shortages were especially salient for district policymakers. Many district policymakers (with the exception of those in the two suburban and the two larger urban school districts) reported that a shortage of funds, staff, and time curtailed their efforts to respond to the standards. The time shortage was especially acute in smaller districts. A rural superintendent remarked, "We need a gift of time in a small district." He elaborated:

> State policy filters down to my school administrative staff, which is only three, and if I've got six initiatives, that means that each one has two initiatives they have to follow. I don't have a curriculum director, which means that each one of the principals or teachers has to be responsible for a facet of the curriculum, and if I use a teacher, then that means direct contact with students is going to be reduced. And our economic base is not of a nature where I can go out and hire a curriculum director.

In this district policymaker's view, limited staff contributed to a scarcity of time for instructional matters.

A similar problem emerged when it came to establishing committees to develop new instructional policies. District policymakers explained that because their teaching staffs were small, they had difficulty staffing districtwide committees. Further, administrators had an assortment of disconnected responsibilities, duties that reduced their time for instructional matters. A single administrator often had to address a mixed bag of issues that ranged from building maintenance to teaching, contributing to a shortage of focused time for instructional policymaking. A rural superintendent summed up the situation: "In a small district . . . you are a little bit of everything. A teacher is also an advisor and is also the coach and is also the driver's ed. instructor . . . And the principal is also this, this, and this . . . you get a lot of very frustrated people . . . The time factor is for all of us getting to be the very big thing." District policymakers did not have the luxury of focusing on instructional issues for sustained periods of time. This time was necessary if district policymakers were to work together, and with outside experts, to understand the reform ideas and figure out what these ideas might entail for instruction.

Like any resource, a key dimension of time is how people use or allocate it. Certainly most local district policymakers believed that they needed more time if they were to revise and successfully implement instructional policies. But how district policymakers used the available time was critical. In high-support districts, district policymakers devoted a great deal of time to figuring out what state and national standards meant. The district allocated time for the policymakers to figure out the instructional ideas pressed by standards. For example, district policymakers in suburban Pleasant Valley decided to postpone writing a mathematics guide because members of the committee argued that they needed more time to learn about the mathematics standards.

Similarly, Riverville's policymakers appreciated that it would take time for them and teachers to figure out the mathematics standards. They made this time available. Riverville's superintendent remarked, "It is not unusual for a district to get an idea and try to slap it together in a year or two and then it goes on a shelf and it dies. It has to be an ongoing, neverending thing." The assistant superintendent explained: "We are talking in terms of years. Not one, two, three years . . . it takes intensive professional development over a concentrated period of time." District policymakers in Riverville had spent seven years working on mathematics reform and were still at it. They had managed to sustain a focus on mathematics instruction over the long haul. As one school principal described, "Our district's approach to training is slow and steady. It's not just one shot, this subject, then that subject." The assistant superintendent elaborated: "We don't bring in this speaker one year and another speaker another year. We try to have an ongoing project. For instance, we've been doing math training for seven years now."

This perspective on time contrasted sharply with that of policymakers in the low-support districts, where surface-level understandings of the standards were the norm. Here, time was typically viewed in terms of meeting procedural requirements. When it came to the allocation and use of time, these procedural concerns typically outweighed and preempted developing deeper understandings of the ideas advanced by standards. District policymakers often hurriedly put together their mathematics or science policies over a single school year or, in a couple of cases, purchased a mathematics guide from a neighboring school district. In rural Woodland, for example, the chair of the district's mathematics committee argued unsuccessfully that more time was needed for committee members to develop a better understanding of the standards before writing new district policies. District administrators insisted, however, that the new mathematics policies needed to be put in place—and their view prevailed. Thus, while some district policymakers viewed time in terms of making deadlines and meeting requirements, others allowed their need to understand the reform ideas to dictate the use of available time.

Thus staffing, time, and materials were important resources for district policymakers' sense-making from and about standards. But while these resources were important, they did not determine the sense-making processes. After all, district policymakers in some small, relatively poor school districts managed to develop deeper understandings of the standards and create district policies that supported these understandings. Some school districts like Riverville managed scarce resources in creative ways, capitalizing on teacher leaders and utilizing connections with external associations to redress time, staffing, and material shortages. The importance of resources such as time, staffing, and materials depended in important measure on human and social resources.

Consider curricular materials. Most districts had either purchased (or were purchasing) new textbooks or curricular materials. But the extent to which these materials contributed to the school-district policymakers' sense of standards varied widely among districts, depending on the school district's human and social resources. Riverville, for example, piloted and adopted a middle-school mathematics curriculum. The adoption of this curriculum, however, involved more than updating the curricular materials. District policymakers used it as an opportunity to develop their understanding of the mathematics standards. District policymakers used the implementation of this new curriculum to focus conversations about the mathematics standards and what they entailed for mathematics teaching and learning. This situation contrasted sharply with that in other districts, where new materials were adopted and teachers were expected to implement them after a workshop or two. In these school districts, district policymakers did not use curricular materials to develop their understanding of the standards. School-district resources for making sense of standards was best understood as the interaction of human, social, and more tangible resources such as time and material.

State Policy and School District Resources for Sense-Making

State policy was influential in district policymakers' sense-making from and about the standards. State policy instruments contributed to getting school-district policymakers to take seriously the mathematics and science standards. As discussed in Chapter 4, state policy, especially state sanctions, motivated district policymakers to try to figure out what standards meant and to develop local policies to support these understandings. State policy instruments, however, also contributed to district policymakers' developing surface-level understandings of the standards.

The Press for Compliance

Michigan's Department of Education lacked the resources to oversee the local implementation of the state's mathematics and science standards. The MDE had to rely on proxies for implementation, requiring each district to file its core curriculum with the state and to publish an annual report. Further, the state's summary accreditation process defined penalties for noncompliance as measured by students' performance on the MEAP. The effectiveness of the state's mandates depended on sanctions and oversight.

While the state's compliance mechanisms motivated district policymakers to attend to instructional policy, in four school districts these requirements focused local policymakers' attention mostly on procedural compliance. Meeting the state-established compliance procedures—having a curriculum guide on file—was the priority. District policymakers in these four districts used available resources to ensure that the paperwork was in order to meet the state's compliance requirements.

Pressed to meet state timelines, these four school districts devoted much of their human and material resources to being in procedural compliance with state policies. An administrator remarked: "I think the state's demands are unrealistic. I don't think there is any consideration given, especially to the smaller districts with limited staff, in regard to meeting deadlines and requirements. It puts a real strain on those districts." In rural Woodland, for example, the chair of the district's mathematics committee argued, with no success, that more time was needed for committee members to develop a better understanding of the mathematics reforms before writing a new curriculum. District administrators, however, wanted to be in compliance with state mandates. The chair explained, "The superintendent and the school board wanted the new updated curriculums in place before the year was over." Procedural compliance took precedence over developing a deeper understanding of the ideas pressed by the mathematics standards.

Of course, school districts could be in compliance but still not have policies that supported the more fundamental changes in mathematics and science education pressed by the standards. One district policymaker noted: "The Public Act 25 verification process is so paperwork oriented . . . it's just so surface-level stuff . . . I've seen districts that have documents and they come out looking beautifully in this verification process but the document is crap, and it sits on a shelf and teachers don't know what's in it and they don't know how to teach it. Those are the problems I have with mandates and the paper." State mandates and inducements demanded compliance; they directed local policymakers to change specific behaviors or to do specific things such as publish an annual school report. They offered district policymakers tangible rewards for following directions and imposed tangible sanctions for failing to do so. But these were blunt instruments. While they may have effectively and efficiently forced district policymakers to file a curriculum (procedural compliance), they were much less effective at getting them to develop deeper-level understandings of the ideas pressed by standards.

A cash-strapped, resource-deprived state education department is in somewhat of a catch-22 when it needs to get the attention of school districts. But in giving their standards clout through easily monitored and affordable procedural requirements, state policymakers may have focused district policymakers' attention unduly on compliance mechanisms rather than on the substance of the state's policy message about mathematics and science education.

Policy Cycles and District Policymakers' Resources for Sense-Making

District policymakers in six districts expressed frustration with the amount of time they had to devote to addressing changes in the state's procedural compliance requirements. They were also exasperated with frequent changes in the rules and regulations that accompanied the state's instructional policies. A district superintendent noted, "We have shuffled and reshuffled some things so many times in my career in education I would hate to even count." Another administrator said, "Public Act 25 keeps changing and that's what we find so aggravating. Just when we think we have things rolling they say, 'Well, no, we're changing this and that.'"

More important, district policymakers reported devoting scarce resources, including time, staff, and money, to figuring out and ensuring their compliance with the latest changes in state regulations.

> Stability over time, oh my! . . . I had to inform my people this year that all the time they took to change their curriculum into outcomes-based language over the last several years is now politically incorrect. Outcomes are out! It's now standards and benchmarks. And I realize it seems like a little thing, but if you knew how much time some of these people took to change the language from objectives to outcomes and now to go back and say, "Oops, never mind the outcomes part" . . . Our professional development money was spent on that.

These problems were compounded in smaller districts, where frequent changes in state regulation had to be managed by one or two district-office staff members:

> This school accreditation is a change from a year ago . . . What was frustrating was in 1989 when P.A. 25 came out I did everything I could to get the education I needed to lead my school . . . I took five full days of training but what I was taught in February and March of '93 was changed in the Christmas package of '93. So here I am telling teachers [that the old goals and strategies are] all out the window now.

Local educators used scarce resources to keep current with procedural changes in state regulations, changes that frequently had little to do with the thrust of the instructional ideas pressed by the state's standards.

Conclusion

Making sense of new knowledge can be taxing. The more the new knowledge departs from current understanding, the more taxing the work. This is as true for district policymakers as it is for any of us. District policymakers' sense-making from and about standards was enabled by human, social, and financial resources. While analytically distinguishable, the nature, activation, and sometimes existence of any of these resources depended on one or more of the others. The school district's human and social resources were influential in district policymakers' activation and use of staff, time, and materials for sense-making from and about the standards. This differential distribution among districts of human, social, and material resources for district policymakers' sense-making was consequential with respect to what ideas about reforming mathematics and science education were constructed from standards and the extent to which the district policies they developed supported the standards.

My account has focused chiefly on school districts and the extent to which their local policymaking initiatives supported state and national standards. An important issue concerns what difference, if any, the level of support district policies provided for state and national standards made for implementation of standards at the classroom level. Do school district policies matter with respect to what teachers do in their mathematics and science lessons? The next two chapters investigate these questions.

CHAPTER 6

The Schoolteacher and Interactive Policymaking

Karen Bedford, a twenty-year veteran of Redwood Public Schools, taught fourth grade at Patterson Elementary. An energetic woman, Bedford reported that she was a changed teacher; she claimed that her mathematics teaching had changed tremendously compared with five years earlier. She depended less on the mathematics textbook and involved her fourth-graders much more in group work. She covered new mathematical content such as geometry, and used more "manipulatives and hands-on activities." Further, she pressed her students to explain and justify their answers and worked hard to refrain from giving them the answers herself. "Bored" and disillusioned with teaching before her transformation, she had reached a point where "I didn't even enjoy coming to school anymore." She explained, "I thought, if I'm bored, the kids must really be hating school because I don't like it and I think as a teacher, you have to be excited to sell it to the kids." These circumstances, coupled with shifts in the thrust of state and district policy, contributed to Bedford working to change her mathematics teaching over a four-year period, changes that made all the difference in the world. As she put it, "I got excited again."

The way Bedford saw it, the state standards, new district policies, and the district's adoption of the Investigations mathematics curriculum were especially influential in the instructional changes she introduced. She added geometry to her curriculum, for example, "because I could see it was on the MEAP." With respect to her teaching strategies, she noted that she was "looking for strategies in math because of the MEAP test." Coursework on mathematics education at a neighboring university, along with Bedford's own efforts to figure out how to get the Investigations mathematics curriculum to work with her students, enabled her to see the importance of group work, manipulatives, and more complex problems in teaching mathematics. This was more than easy talk on Bedford's part. Observing her mathematics teaching, I saw evidence of group work, manipulative use, instruction in geometry, and students working on mathematical problems.

Schoolteachers are the vital agents of implementation. Teachers like Karen Bedford decide ultimately whether and in what ways policy proposals get worked out in classroom practice. If the only policy that matters is that which the client—America's children—receives, then what teachers do in their classrooms is critical. What children receive by way of mathematics and science education depends ultimately on schoolteachers who, in negotiation with their students, deliver instruction.

The Schoolteacher and Instructional Advice

Instructional Policy and Classroom Work

Government policy, especially school-district policy, was the most important source of instructional guidance for teachers. A suburban teacher remarked:

This year I am more structured, I guess, about making sure I do science every day or at least four days out of the week . . . because there has been more push for us to teach more science from our district science frameworks people and from our district curriculum director. Not necessarily from the principal or anyone like the superintendent. It's mostly from people like the curriculum director and the people that are involved in frameworks, who are saying that ideally you should teach science at least forty minutes every day.

District policy encouraged this teacher to teach science more frequently and regularly. Accounts by teachers, especially elementary teachers, suggest that their school districts were important in getting them to teach science and broaden what counted as science education beyond an exclusive focus on biological science. Considering that content coverage is a critical predictor of student achievement, this was a considerable accomplishment.

Other teachers reported that their school districts also influenced the materials they used and their teaching approach. An urban elementary teacher noted:

We have been fortunate in Redwood that we have Olivia; she is our math and science district coordinator . . . But she has been in-servicing us in different areas. And we receive the materials from her. I did a big unit on the planet, for science. I did a big unit with plants . . . So a lot of things we are getting from her already in a box or already in a container; all we have to do is plan them and do them in our classroom. That has really made it a lot easier for me to do a lot of science activities.

The provision by the school district of prepared materials for teaching science enabled this elementary teacher and others we

Table 6.1 Teachers' main source of instructional advice

In planning mathematics lessons, what is your main source of written information when . . .	MEAP for mathematics	NCTM Professional Teaching Standards (1991)	NCTM Curriculum and Evaluation Standards (1989)	Your school district's mathematics curriculum or objectives	Michigan Essential Goals and Objectives for Mathematics Education
1. Deciding which topics to teach (goals)?	25%	2%	2%	62%	9%
2. Deciding how to present a topic?	24%	3%	3%	62%	9%
3. Selecting problems and exercises for work in class and homework?	21%	3%	3%	69%	6%
4. Selecting problems and applications for assessment and evaluation?	36%	2%	2%	53%	7%

interviewed, who believed they were not knowledgeable about science, to acquire the necessary materials to teach science.*

The situation was similar for mathematics. Teachers reported that their school district's efforts to reform mathematics education through professional development, curriculum frameworks, and district leaders' formal and informal communication with teachers were important influences on their teaching. A suburban teacher noted, "We have district objectives that we're responsible for that pretty much drive my curriculum as far as math. Also we were given lots of manipulatives." An urban teacher explained: "It started here in the Redwood school district where the head of math talked a lot about using manipulatives and getting the kids to visualize, to see these things and to touch them. And so I started changing to using a lot of manipulatives after going to those in-services, and then I've gone to other in-services."

Overall, teachers systematically reported that they were guided more by district curriculum mandates than state or national standards. More than 60 percent of the teachers reported that their school district's curriculum for mathematics education was their most important source of written information in deciding both which topics to teach and how to present a topic (see Table 6.1). Nearly seven out of ten teachers identified their school district's curriculum for mathematics education as their primary source when selecting classroom work and homework in mathematics. When it came to selecting problems and applications for assessment and evaluation of students, over half of the teachers identified the school district as their primary source for information.

Some state policy instruments also figured prominently for teachers, most notably the state assessment program (MEAP).

---

* While the survey did not ask teachers about their primary source of information for their science teaching, we did talk with the subsample of thirty-two teachers we selected for observation and for interviews about influences on their science teaching.

One teacher explained with respect to content coverage, "I'm making assumptions based on what I know is on the MEAP test." Another teacher explained that she focused on problem solving because students would be tested on their problem-solving ability when they took the MEAP: "Kids are specifically responsible for problem-solving strategies . . . it's on the MEAP. It's something I need to zero in on so that they've had some exposure and feel comfortable with it." In deciding what topics to teach, a quarter of the teachers identified the state's mathematics student assessment program (MEAP) as their main source of advice. Teachers also spoke about the importance of MEAP in influencing their approach to teaching science. One teacher remarked: "The buck stops with me. Because the MEAP test says they have to be able to do a lab from start to finish, that was my goal . . . to get them ready for that." This teacher taught students to do science experiments because they would be tested on this when they took the new state assessment for science.

The situation was similar with respect to teaching strategies for mathematics. As one teacher said, "I'm very interested now in looking for strategies in reading and math because of the MEAP test." Another teacher explained that the expectation that students use multiple representations in reporting their answers and explaining their answers on the MEAP influenced her approach to teaching mathematics: "Yes, the students are going to be expected to not just give an answer, but explain how they got it [in pictures and words]." Another teacher remarked: "That's one of the goals . . . trying to expose them more to the pictorial things. Because the tests are basically pictorial." Again, almost one-quarter of the teachers reported that when deciding how to present a topic, the state's assessment system was their primary source of written information. As one might expect, the relevance of the MEAP increased when it came to selecting problems and applications for assessment and evaluation of students, with more than a third of

Table 6.2 Teachers' familiarity with documents overall

Indicate your familiarity with each of the following documents:	No such document	Not familiar	Fairly familiar	Very familiar
Mathematics				
1. National Council of Teachers of Mathematics (NCTM) Curriculum and Evaluation Standards	1%	51%	36%	12%
2. National Council of Teachers of Mathematics (NCTM) Professional Teaching Standards	1%	59%	29%	11%
3. Michigan Essential Goals and Objectives for Mathematics Education	1%	23%	48%	29%
4. Your school district's mathematics curriculum guide or objectives	2%	2%	29%	67%
5. Michigan Educational Assessment Program (MEAP) for mathematics	1%	3%	32%	65%
6. American Association for the Advancement of Science's (AAAS) Science for All Americans	2%	82%	13%	3%
7. Michigan Essential Goals and Objectives for Science Education (MEGOSE)	1%	44%	34%	21%
8. Your school district's science curriculum or science objectives	2%	8%	37%	52%
9. Michigan Educational Assessment Program (MEAP) for science	1%	14%	43%	43%

the teachers identifying it as their primary source for information.

Teachers also reported considerable familiarity with the mathematics and science standards, especially as represented in state and school-district policy documents. Ninety-six percent of the teachers reported being either fairly or very familiar with their district's policies about mathematics education, while almost 90 percent reported being so for science (see Table 6.2). They also indicated being familiar with state policy documents, especially the

MEAP for mathematics and for science. Over 95 percent of the teachers reported being either fairly or very familiar with the MEAP for mathematics, while 86 percent noted being either fairly or very familiar with the science MEAP. With respect to the state's essential goals and objectives for mathematics, over 75 percent of the teachers reported being either fairly or very familiar with them. Teachers were not nearly as familiar with the state's science standards: nearly 45 percent of teachers indicated that they were not familiar.

State and local school-district policy, then, was an especially important source of information about mathematics instruction for teachers. While the school district did not have a monopoly on advising teachers about their mathematics instruction, it was the single most important source of guidance.

Though not nearly as prominent for teachers as state and local policy, the professional sector was also influential, especially with respect to mathematics education. Almost 50 percent of the teachers reported that they were fairly or very familiar with the Curriculum and Evaluation Standards created by the National Council of Teachers of Mathematics (NCTM).

District Policy as Surrogate

While school-district policy was the main source of advice for most teachers, singling out one policy and attempting to gauge its independent import for teachers fails to capture how different levels of the policy system interacted to influence teachers' work. Teachers' accounts suggest that policies worked together rather than in isolation to influence their practice. Moreover, because most teachers relied primarily on district instructional policies for guidance about their mathematics and science teaching, school-district policy became a surrogate for state and national standards.

Different levels of the system—the state, the national standards, the school district, and the school—worked in tandem to influence instruction. Specifically, the salience of state policy for classroom teachers was amplified by the school district. District policymakers used state policy to leverage school administrators and teachers to attend to district instructional policies. The salience of both district and state policy in turn was magnified for teachers by school principals and school-level policies. Teachers explained:

> You go nowhere without saying the word "MEAP" . . . You know, when your back is up against the wall, you have got to do something, and of course the district administration puts pressure on the principal, the principal on the teachers.

> The district is really putting pressure on the principals. The principals are feeling the most pressure . . . they need to come up with strategies that will improve the scores at their building level, or they may find their selves in big trouble . . . transferred into other positions, or demoted. I think they're putting a lot of pressure on them . . . That's the pressure the teachers were feeling.

> What our school leader focuses on is: "Are we following our state objectives?" "How are we assessing those objectives?" "How can we assess how well we are teaching?" "Are we teaching what we say we are teaching?" We are accountable. And at the end of the year we turn in those state objectives, and we tell how we taught every single one.

For these teachers, the MEAP, as mediated by their school districts and their school administrators, was especially influential in their work. The significance of state-level policies such as the MEAP was increased by the actions of policymakers and administrators at lower levels of the school system. State, district, and school-level instructional initiatives worked together to influence teachers' classroom practice.

As the single most important source of guidance for teachers about their instruction, district policy became the mathematics and science standards for most teachers. Relying on district policies about mathematics and science instruction, teachers believed they were responding to state (and in some cases national) standards. But, as documented in Chapter 3, the ideas about mathematics and science education supported by school district policies varied among districts. In particular, districts differed with respect to how much their policies supported core elements of the standards; most districts failed to develop policies that supported transforming what counted as mathematics and science knowledge and how mathematics and science were taught in school. Hence teachers, who relied chiefly on their school district's policies for guidance about teaching to the standards, received rather different advice depending on their school district. As a stand-in for state and national standards, district policies mattered because they became the standards for most teachers.

Positioning the Person in Policy Analysis

In analyzing the progress of policy in practice, it is easy to lose the person; the policy becomes all encompassing. As Karen Bedford's case reminds us, however, policy implementation is about people. In Bedford's case, her boredom with teaching was an important reason why she sought to transform her mathematics instruction. She needed to change. She was not alone. Other teachers like Laura Reston, a committed elementary schoolteacher for twenty years, expressed similar sentiments:

> I really was going through a period [when] I said I liked teaching because I liked kids, but I really was sort of bored myself. And when I changed this way it renewed for me an interest in teaching. So it was not difficult at all to change. I was really glad to do it because after twenty, well, sixteen at that time, years of

teaching it was like starting over again and it gave me kind of a renewed feeling.

While district and state policies were influential in Bedford's and Reston's cases, they worked together with more personal factors—where teachers were in their careers, for example, or their need to revive their interest in teaching.

Teachers also referred to their own experiences in school as influential in their efforts to reconsider their teaching practice. Take Tina Ingle, a middle-school science teacher in Pleasant Valley. While district and state policy were especially influential in Ingle's efforts to revise her science teaching, her own experience in school was also tremendously important. She recalled: "I was a very good student, but I hated school. I'm a kinesthetic learner and I never remember putting my hands on anything for lab. Nothing. I mean, science was all out of a book. It was just a huge major disappointment to me and I just hated school . . . And so all along I have always tried to look for a way that the kids can be actively involved in what they are doing. But I didn't always know." For Ingle, state and district policies about science education reinforced her personal conviction that students needed to be actively involved in doing scientific inquiry. To attend to the person in policy analysis is not to negate the social or organizational dimensions of teachers' efforts to make sense of and implement the standards. It is merely to acknowledge that teachers do not take advice from standards as blank slates but rather as people with experiences and knowledge that are consequential to their sense-making.

Something Old and Something New

Teachers reported that the mathematics and science standards, especially as represented in local school-district policies, were an important source of guidance on instruction. We might conclude, then, that the mathematics and sciences standards were a success in that they garnered considerable attention from classroom teachers. But, such a conclusion would be premature. At a minimum, to gauge the success of the standards we have to explore the extent to which what teachers did in the classroom was consistent with the ideas about mathematics and science education pressed by the standards.

Teachers' Beliefs

One measure of the influence of standards on teachers' work can be obtained from examining teachers' beliefs. Teachers' beliefs are an important influence on their teaching.* Hence, teachers who view mathematics exclusively in terms of procedural knowledge will differ in how they present mathematics to students compared with teachers who appreciate mathematics as involving principled knowledge.

Results from the survey we conducted suggest that teachers' thinking aligned with reform concepts. When asked, "To be good in mathematics at school, how important do you think it is for students to . . . ?", teachers overwhelmingly identified statements that were consistent with the mathematics standards as being very important (see Table 6.3). Specifically, nine in ten teachers thought that it was very important for students to "understand mathematical concepts, principles, and strategies" and to "understand how mathematics is used in the real world." Over 80 percent of teachers felt that it was important that students "be able to provide reasons to support their solutions." Teachers strongly endorsed those statements that supported the sort of mathematics instruction urged by the standards. Further, the more conventional idea about mathematics as remembering formulas and

---

* The survey asked teachers about their beliefs only about mathematics instruction.

Table 6.3 Teachers' ideas about reform and conventional teaching overall

"To be good in mathematics at school, how important do you think it is for students to . . ."	Not important	Somewhat important	Very important
Reform ideas			
1. Understand mathematical concepts, principles, and strategies?	0%	8%	92%
2. Understand how mathematics is used in the real world?	0%	11%	89%
3. Be able to provide reasons to support their solutions?	0%	16%	85%
Conventional ideas			
4. Remember formulas and procedures?	8%	49%	43%

procedures was deemed very important by only 43 percent of the teachers.

Taken together, these findings suggest that the ideas about reforming mathematics instruction pressed by the standards had gained currency with teachers. Caution is necessary in interpreting these data. Some teachers may already have subscribed to these ideas prior to their encounters with state and national standards. Hence we cannot take these data as evidence that the mathematics standards influenced teachers' beliefs. Still, most of the teachers we interviewed suggested that their ideas about mathematics and science instruction had changed over the past few years, albeit they did not always tie these changes directly to standards.

Instructional Practice

Another way of appraising the influence of standards on teachers' work is to examine teachers' reports of their classroom practices. Most teachers reported instruction that involved a hybrid of conventional and standards-oriented practices. Many teachers, often a majority, reported teaching mathematics and science in ways that approximated some aspects of the mathematics and science standards in at least some lessons and often in most or all lessons. At the same time, these teachers reported continuing to engage in some conventional instructional practices that the standards sought to change.

With respect to mathematics education, teachers' reports about the mathematics tasks that students worked on, their treatment of students' ideas, and their grouping arrangements suggest that some standards-oriented practices were implemented much more widely than others (see Table 6.4). As discussed in Chapter 2, the mathematics standards emphasized that students should do more than simply compute the correct answer: they should explain and justify their answers. Students were to have opportunities to "speak mathematics" so that they could clarify their thinking, appreciate different ways of representing mathematical ideas, and learn about doing mathematics. More than six in ten teachers reported that they had students "explain the reasoning behind an idea" in most or every lesson (see item 1 in Table 6.4). One teacher explained that her students "do a lot of discussion" because "it gives them the ability to question and explain their thinking." Another teacher noted how the push to get students to explain their thinking represented considerable change in her teaching. "I have to be constantly . . . working to pull their ideas out . . . Before they could have just given me the answer, but it was the answer for the wrong reason. Now they are explaining everything." Fewer than 2 percent of the teachers reported that they never or almost never had students explain their reasoning.

Calculator use is another indicator of reformed practice, albeit a rather weak indicator on its own. What is key is whether and *how* calculators are used. The survey attempted to get at this by asking teachers how often students used calculators for "exploring number concepts." Again, teachers' reports suggest that their practice was relatively consistent with the sort of practices promoted by the standards. Almost 70 percent of the teachers in our

Table 6.4 Teachers' reports of their mathematics instruction

Teachers' reports	Never or almost never	Some lessons	Most or every lesson
"In your mathematics lessons, how often do you usually ask students to . . ."			
1. Explain the reasoning behind an idea?	1%	35%	64%
2. Work on problems for which there is no immediately obvious method of solution?	38%	56%	6%
3. Practice computational skills?	2%	35%	63%
"In mathematics lessons, how often do students . . ."			
4. Work individually without assistance from the teacher?	25%	58%	17%
5. Work individually with assistance from the teacher?	2%	58%	41%
6. Work together as a class with the teacher teaching the whole class?	4%	49%	47%
7. Work together as a class with students responding to one another?	6%	64%	30%
8. Work in pairs or small groups without assistance from the teacher?	19%	65%	16%
9. Work in pairs or small groups with assistance from the teacher?	1%	66%	34%

sample reported having students use calculators to explore number concepts at least once or twice a month (see Table 6.5). Further, 70 percent of the teachers reported having students use calculators to solve complex problems at least once or twice a month. Indeed, 27 percent of the teachers reported engaging in this practice at least once or twice a week. Of course, without knowing whether respondents understood number concepts as involving principled mathematical knowledge or how they defined complex problems, it is difficult to gauge the extent to which this practice mirrors the larger goals of the mathematics standards.

Table 6.5 Teachers' calculator practices overall

"How often do students in your class use calculators for the following activities?"	Never, or hardly ever	Once or twice a month	Once or twice a week	Almost every day
1. Checking answers	38%	38%	18%	7%
2. Tests and exams	74%	19%	5%	2%
3. Routine computation	42%	39%	15%	5%
4. Solving complex problems	30%	43%	20%	7%
5. Exploring number concepts	27%	48%	19%	6%

Other standards-oriented practices did not figure as prominently in the classroom practices reported by these teachers, though they still were present. Problem solving, as discussed in Chapter 2, was another key organizing tenet of the mathematics standards. While fewer than 10 percent of the teachers reported having students work on mathematics problems for which there were no immediately obvious methods of solution in most or every lesson, more than 55 percent reported engaging students with these sorts of problems in at least some lessons. Still, almost 40 percent of the teachers reported that they never or almost never involved their students in the sort of mathematical problem solving pressed by the mathematics standards.

Teacher interview data suggest that while problem solving involved changing teachers' mathematics instruction, for most it did not involve the sort of dramatic change pressed by the mathematics standards. An elementary teacher explained, "When I began teaching problem solving I was just doing algorithms, learning to multiply and divide fractions . . . but what we do now is put problem solving in a real-life context." Another teacher remarked, "I wanted them to try to make the connection between the story problem and their multiplication. And then tie that in with what we saw yesterday on the field trip." Another teacher noted, "We do so much problem solving . . . We do one problem a week and we have nine strategies. 'Guess and check.' 'Make an organized list.' There are about ten or twelve strategies that we teach them and as a matter of fact each morning they have a math problem . . . Today they had 'Rich needs forty hot dog buns for the party. The buns are sold in packages of six. How many packages should Rich buy?' So we used division." For these teachers, problem solving in mathematics did represent a fundamental change and went beyond the conventional story problems that are a mainstay of mathematics classrooms. Their takes on problem solving, however, did not involve some core aspects pressed by the mathematics standards—in particular, problems for which the solutions are not immediately obvious and that do not lend themselves to the wholesale application of ready-made procedures (NCTM, 1989).

A similar pattern was evident with respect to science instruction. More than six in ten teachers reported that they had students "explain the reasoning behind an idea" in most or every lesson (see item 1 in Table 6.6). More than nine in ten teachers had students do this in at least some lessons. Just over half of the teachers who responded to the survey reported that they had students "write explanations about what was observed and why it happened" either in most lessons or in every lesson. More than nine in ten teachers had students complete this task in at least some lessons. Finally, although it was not a regular feature of science instruction, more than nine in ten teachers who responded to the survey claimed that they had students put events or objects in order and give a reason for the organization in at least some lessons.

Grouping arrangements in both mathematics and science classrooms also represented a blend of more conventional and standards-oriented practices. The mathematics and science standards encouraged the creation of opportunities for students to work together on mathematics and science problems so that students would learn to reason with one another about their ideas. For this to happen, grouping students for instruction would have to change from the conventional arrangements of individual seatwork or whole-class lessons in which students interacted only with the teacher rather than with their peers. Teachers' reports suggest that the ideas about grouping arrangements pressed by standards were used by most teachers in at least some lessons. More than nine in ten teachers reported that they had students work together as a class with students responding to one another in both science and mathematics lessons in at least some lessons. Similarly, seven in ten teachers reported that for both their science and mathematics instruction, they had students work in

Table 6.6 Teachers' reports of their science instruction

Teachers' reports	Never or almost never	Some lessons	Most or every lesson
"In your science lessons, how often do you usually ask students to . . ."			
Explain the reasoning behind an idea?	1%	34%	65%
Write explanations about what was observed and why it happened?	6%	41%	53%
Put events or objects in order and give a reason for the organization?	8%	64%	28%
"In science lessons, how often do students . . ."			
Work individually without assistance from the teacher?	42%	55%	4%
Work individually with assistance from the teacher?	11%	75%	14%
Work together as a class with the teacher teaching the whole class?	3%	60%	37%
Work together as a class with students responding to one another?	9%	61%	30%
Work in pairs or small groups without assistance from the teacher?	23%	66%	11%
Work in pairs or small groups with assistance from the teacher?	2%	61%	36%

pairs or small groups (with teacher assistance) in at least some lessons. Teachers reported blending these grouping arrangements with more conventional individual seatwork. For example, nearly nine in ten teachers reported that they had students work individually with their assistance in at least some mathematics and science lessons. At the same time, three-quarters of the teachers reported having students work individually without their assistance in at least some mathematics lessons. While standards-oriented grouping arrangements were popular in these classrooms, conventional grouping arrangements continued to have a stronghold on teachers' practice, especially in mathematics.

Overall, teachers' reports of their classroom practice suggest that they were teaching mathematics and science in ways that were consistent with at least some elements of the standards. Some of these elements, however, were more prevalent than others, so the ideas about instruction encouraged by the standards appear to have progressed unevenly in these classrooms. Further, standards-oriented practices were blended with more conventional approaches to mathematics and science instruction.

At one level, these accounts suggest something of a success story. Although we cannot attribute the practices reported by teachers to the standards, many of the instructional practices they reported were roughly consistent with those pressed by the mathematics and science education standards. Moreover, these teachers' reports, when contrasted with the mathematics instruction reported by previous research undertaken in the late 1970s and 1980s, suggest substantial differences in mathematics and science education. For example, the modal instruction captured by these studies portrayed a K–8 mathematics curriculum focused almost entirely on basic skills, and mostly on basic operations and rudiments of geometry (Goodlad, 1984; Porter, 1989; Stake and Easley, 1978). According to these studies, teachers often paid little attention to mathematical concepts or problem solving, typically either lecturing to the class or monitoring students' written work. Students spent most of their time on pencil-and-paper mathematics, filling out workbooks and worksheets. A distinctly different portrayal of mathematics and science instruction emerges from our study, which was carried out a couple of decades later.

Some caution is in order when interpreting these accounts. While surveys offer insights on classroom practice, they also have limits (Mayer, 1999). To begin with, field studies have identified considerable discrepancies between teachers' reports about their practice and the practice observed by researchers in these teachers' classrooms. Aside from the problems with teachers' self-reports, the survey items are ambiguous, especially with respect to the academic content of the classroom tasks and the discourse patterns. For example, while as mentioned earlier more than six in ten teachers reported getting students to explain the reasoning behind their ideas in most or every mathematics lesson, it is difficult to tell from this response the substance of this reasoning. Did these teachers press students to reason about principled mathematical knowledge, or was the reasoning mostly about procedural knowledge? Did student reasoning in these classrooms involve anything more than being able to list the steps in a memorized computational procedure? We will return to this issue in Chapter 7.

Classroom Instruction and How Teachers Take Advice

One issue concerns the relations between teachers' sources of advice about mathematics and science education and the extent to which their mathematics and science instruction approximated the ideas encouraged by standards. Considering that school-district policies were the single most important source of guidance about instruction for most teachers, one would expect some relationship between teachers' classroom practice and the ideas about instruction in their districts' instructional policies. Specifically, were teachers in the high-support school districts for the mathematics and/or science standards (as discussed in Chapters 3 and 4) teaching in ways that more closely approximated the standards than were teachers in the six school districts that offered low support for the standards? It is important to remember that my goal in creating this book was to develop some tenable hypotheses about relations between national, state, and district policymaking and teachers' instruction, hypotheses that could be tested in future work.*

Answering the question of whether teachers' knowledge of and

---

* Questions of effects are difficult because one has to identify and support a causal relation, and causality is difficult to determine. Indeed, absent a randomized experiment, it is difficult to support a causal relationship, and randomization is frequently (though not always) difficult with public policy. My purpose, then, was not to show that district policies caused teachers to practice in ways that were more or less in line with the standards.

Table 6.7 Regression model: teacher innovation as a dependent variable for high- and low-support math districts

Teacher innovation	High-support districts		Low-support districts	
	B	Std. error	B	Std. error
Familiarity with NCTM Curriculum Standards (1989)	.088	(.226)	.025	(.263)
Familiarity with NCTM Teaching Standards (1991)	.331	(.225)	.53*	(.290)
Familiarity with Michigan Essential Goals and Objectives for Mathematics Education	.021	(.205)	.181	(.168)
Familiarity with your school district's mathematics curriculum guide or objectives	.524*	(.273)	.021	(.196)
Familiarity with National Assessment for Educational Progress (NAEP) Assessment Framework/Specifications	.136	(.283)	−.249	(.243)
Familiarity with Michigan Educational Assessment Program (MEAP) for Mathematics	.553**	(.251)	.233	(.219)
Reliance on your own previously prepared lessons	−.059	(.157)	−.022	(.121)
Reliance on a written plan compiled by teachers in the school	−.087	(.196)	−.075	(.147)
Reliance on other teachers or math specialists in your school/department	.423**	(.212)	.135	(.177)
Reliance on student textbooks	−.097	(.183)	−.708***	(.195)
Reliance on other textbooks or resource books	−.076	(.171)	.154	(.159)
Reliance on teacher guides or teacher edition of textbook	−.151	(.133)	.446**	(.205)
Reliance on external examinations or standardized tests	.063	(.155)	−.177	(.163)

* Significant at the $p < .10$ level
** Significant at the $p < .05$ level
*** Significant at the $p < .01$ level

attitudes toward reform differ between low-support and high-support districts required that we construct a scale of "standards-oriented instruction" and relate it to district policy using regression analysis. The Appendix contains details on scales and the analysis.

My analysis suggests a relationship between the level of district support for standards and the extent to which teachers' practice was consistent with the standards. For the three school districts whose policies provided high support for the mathematics standards, teacher familiarity with their district's mathematics curriculum guide was a significant predictor of standards-oriented instruction in mathematics (see Table 6.7). In contrast, teacher familiarity with their district's mathematics curriculum guide was not a significant predictor of standards-oriented instruction in the six districts whose policies provide low support for the mathematics standards.

The situation was similar for science. In the three school districts where district policies provided high support for the science standards, teacher familiarity with the district science curriculum guide was a significant predictor of standards-oriented instruction (see Table 6.8). As one might expect, teacher familiarity with the district's science curriculum guide was not a significant predictor of standards-oriented instruction in the six districts that provided low support for the science standards. These analyses, coupled with the earlier analysis, suggest that school districts do matter when it comes to the classroom implementation of standards. When district policies are designed to support state and national standards, they enable classroom-level implementation of the standards.

But school districts were not the whole story: other variables also mattered. In the three school districts that provided high support for the mathematics standards, teacher familiarity with the state assessment for mathematics (MEAP) was also a significant predictor of standards-oriented instruction in mathe-

Table 6.8 Regression model: teacher innovation as a dependent variable for high-support science districts

Teacher innovation	B	Std. error
American Association for Advancement of Science's (AAAS) Science for All Americans	.159	(.239)
Michigan Essential Goals and Objectives for Science Education (MEGOSE)	.168	(.146)
Your school district's science curriculum or science objectives	.473*	(.225)
Michigan Educational Assessment Program (MEAP) for Science	.039	(.177)

* Significant at the p < .05 level

matics (see Table 6.7). Further, teachers' reliance on other teachers or math specialists in their school or department was also a significant predictor of standards-oriented instruction in mathematics. Hence, the school or subject-matter department in middle schools was also influential.

In some instances, school and / or department-level initiatives served to amplify district policy messages. Teachers work in schools, and it is common knowledge that schools differ within districts: some are led well and others poorly; some have cultures that support experimentation, while others lean toward the status quo. For example, at Mason Middle School in suburban Pleasant Valley, teachers in the mathematics department worked through the district curriculum at more or less the same pace. They sometimes worked together to design common tests, worksheets, and homework assignments. Cary Baxter, a fourth-year teacher in the department, explained, "In this school you have to understand we work together quite closely to begin with . . . Last year there were two of us that were teaching the eight point two class. And we would sit down and we would plan out what we we're going to do for this chapter, this unit." In this way school and departmental cultures both contributed to amplifying district policy and provided opportunities for teachers to work together on figuring out how best to implement the policy.

Of course, some school or department cultures did little to amplify district policy messages or create opportunities for teachers to make sense of these messages. For example, in Riverville, where the district initiatives provided strong support for state and national standards in mathematics, the principal of one of the district's two elementary schools was not an avid supporter of the district's policies about mathematics education. Instead he saw his role as buffering his teachers from the district's "math mafia." Some teachers in this school resisted going to the district-organized staff development session on mathematics.

For the six school districts that provided low support for the mathematics standards, teachers' familiarity with the National Council of Teachers of Mathematics' Teaching Standards and their reliance on teacher guides or teacher editions of the mathematics textbook were also significant predictors of standards-oriented mathematics instruction (see Table 6.7). There was as well a significant negative relationship between teachers' reliance on the student textbook and standards-oriented practice. Teachers who reported relying more on the student textbook reported less standards-oriented mathematics instruction. With respect to science instruction, teachers' familiarity with their school districts' science curriculum guide was the only significant predictor of standards-oriented instruction and was only significant in the three school districts where district policies provided high support for the science standards.

Conclusion

State standards, as mediated by district policy, did reach classroom teachers. Teachers paid attention to and took advice about their mathematics and science teaching from these policies. District policies were important counsel for teachers. For most teachers, their school district's instructional policies became the mathematics and science standards. While the district was not the only source from which teachers took advice about instruction, it was the most prominent. Yet although districts were important, and exerted an influence on teachers, they did so in different ways. The notions about mathematics and science that district policies supported varied considerably among districts and were not always consistent with state and national standards. When district policymakers initiated policies that supported only surface-level understandings of the standards, they limited the opportunities within the formal school system for teachers to make sense of those standards. By contrast, when district policymakers initiated policies that nurtured deeper-level understandings of the standards, they created opportunities for teachers to make sense of the mathematics and science standards on this more substantive level. By virtue of the ideas about instruction that district policies support, school districts can selectively, and unintentionally, edge out some ideas advanced by state and national standards. District policymakers can in this way unwittingly interfere with the classroom-level implementation of standards. Indeed, the success of state and national standards at the classroom level depended in important measure on district policymaking.

Nevertheless, some teachers in school districts that provided only low support for standards did report high levels of classroom implementation. These teachers did so by marshalling resources beyond the school district, such as the NCTM standards. This might account for the NCTM standards being a significant predictor of standards-oriented teaching in low-support districts. These teachers, however, more than likely expend a considerable amount of their own resources in the process.

The influence of district policies on classroom-level implementation of the standards was mediated by other factors, ranging from those within the school to those beyond in the broader policy systems. One way to think about relations among state and national standards, school-district policy, and classroom practice is to imagine a regression equation that predicts classroom implementation of the standards. This equation would include variables that fall under "state standards," "school," "school district," "national standards," and "teachers' knowledge and experiences," among other categories. In this equation, the district variables (for example, high versus low support for standards), indeed each variable, would be interdependent rather than independent. The value of any one variable in predicting implementation would depend in some part on the other variables. For example, one could find relatively high levels of implementation in a classroom where a teacher had developed deep knowledge of the standards in her preservice education, but where district policies and programs reflected a low level of support for standards. School districts matter, but how they matter depends on other factors.

My analysis suggests that classroom teachers do heed instructional policies, especially local school-district policies. Moreover, teachers attempted in good faith to incorporate the ideas they understood from these policies into their practice, even though some teachers were much more successful at this than others. In this respect, my account contrasts with work that depicts classrooms as decoupled from policy, and suggests something of a success story for education policy, especially when compared with the doom-and-gloom tenor of the policy implementation literature. The extent to which school-district policies about instruction support the standards is important in accounting for classroom-level variability in the implementation of standards. The classroom-level implementation of standards is addressed more closely in the next chapter.

CHAPTER 7

Policy in Practice

Eₗᵢᵤₐ... Eₗᵢₐbₑₜₕ Tₒᵣᵧ, a teacher of eighteen years, taught fourth-graders in Riverville. Her twenty-seven fourth-graders, most of whom she described as "below average readers," were seated in groups of four around a spacious classroom. In Tory's opinion, mathematics was neither her strength nor passion; she loved to teach social studies.

During one lesson Tory had her students work on "Jessie's problem": "Jessie said that three-quarters and five-sixths are the same size because they both have one piece missing. Do you agree? Explain. Use pictures to make your argument clear." After students had worked on the problem for approximately twenty-five minutes, the remainder of the class was devoted to students sharing, justifying, and critiquing each other's solutions. Much of the discussion centered around one student's justification for concluding that Jessie was right. The student, Ron, drew two rectangles of different lengths on the blackboard, dividing one into four equal pieces and shading in three of the pieces while dividing the other into six and shading in five pieces—something like this:

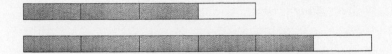

Ron noted, "This is showing three-quarters," pointing to the smaller rectangle. Pointing to the larger rectangle he noted, "and that's five-sixths." Tory listened and then said to the class, "Some of you say 'no' to Ron's idea. Why?" Other students immediately objected and the teacher proceeded to facilitate a discussion among students about the "whole" when comparing fractions.

A nineteen-year veteran teacher, Nancy Isaro taught fourth-graders at Falcon Elementary in Pleasant Valley, a prosperous suburban neighborhood. Isaro's twenty-five fourth-graders were clustered in groups of five around a large classroom. Isaro enjoyed both mathematics and science, serving on Falcon's mathematics task force and having responsibility for teaching science in all fourth-grade classrooms.

Isaro began one lesson with a story problem: "At Tuff's diner you get a free lunch after buying eight lunches. If you ate the lunch at Tuff's forty-five times last year, how many of those lunches were free?" After students had worked for ten minutes on their own, Isaro asked for the answer. Stacie supplied an answer, saying, "It's forty-five divided by eight, which equals five remainder five." Isaro inquired, "First, what operation did you use?" "Division," Stacie responded. Acknowledging the correctness of Stacie's answer, Isaro went on to note, "I am interested in operations. The problem says that you have to eat eight times before you get one free meal. So, it's eight plus one because the ninth meal is free. So, it would be nine into forty-five." Isaro spent the remainder of the lesson teaching students to apply the long-division procedure accurately.

Both Tory and Isaro were familiar with the mathematics standards and were convinced that they were teaching mathematics in ways that resonated with the standards. For both, mathematical "problem solving" was central in their efforts to revise their mathematics instruction over the past few years.

Still, what students could learn about mathematical problem solving was very different in these two classrooms. Although the mathematics embedded in the Tuff's diner problem was more complex than the mathematics in the Jessie problem, Isaro was concerned exclusively with the procedural mathematical knowledge. Problem solving was chiefly an occasion for practicing computational skills. Focusing on getting students to apply the long-division procedure accurately, Isaro framed the lesson in a way that failed to bring to the surface the principled mathematical knowledge embedded in the problem. In contrast, Tory's students' experience with problem solving was centered on principled mathematical knowledge: doing mathematics involved justifying solutions and the strategies used to arrive at those solutions. She set up the Jessie problem to show students that fractions are always a reference to a whole and that this whole is critical when comparing fractions. Further, she framed the problem so that students had to justify their ideas.

Neither Isaro nor Tory was trying to deceive us in reporting about their mathematics teaching. Both believed they were doing problem solving in ways that were consistent with the standards. What it meant to engage in and be good at mathematical problem solving, however, looked very different in these two classrooms.

For policy analysts, figuring out whether a policy succeeded or failed is central. To gauge the success of standards it is necessary to examine whether teachers did something by way of "carrying out" the standards and the extent to which that something was consistent with policymakers' intentions. Both Isaro and Tory did much to revise their practices and carry out the standards. I now take a closer look at this issue by presenting the results of my study of twenty-five teachers, including Isaro and Tory, who reported that they were teaching in ways aligned with the mathematics standards (see Appendix).

The Uneven Progress of Standards in Practice

There was considerable evidence of mathematics practice that supported the standards in the twenty-five classrooms. These teachers emphasized problem solving in mathematics. They worked to tie the mathematics they taught to the real world. They used multiple representations. They used a variety of concrete materials to teach mathematics. And they used a combination of whole-class, small-group, and individual instruction.

Though striking, these similarities cloaked significant differences. As discussed in Chapter 2, it is imperative to examine what counted as mathematical knowledge and doing mathematics in the tasks that students worked on and the conversations they had about these tasks. After all, a teacher might give students tasks with more mathematical problems to be solved in small groups while making no changes to the mathematical content of those tasks. The mathematical tasks might remain firmly grounded in procedural mathematical knowledge.

There were striking differences among classrooms with respect to the mathematical tasks students worked on and the discourse they engaged in around these tasks. These differences are illuminated when we contrast Isaro's and Tory's classrooms. Both used story problems in their mathematics lessons. Both took the mathematics standards seriously. Both teachers claimed that the practice we observed was representative of their efforts to incorporate problem solving into their mathematics instruction. Yet their understandings and enactments of problem solving looked distinctly different.

Tory, as discussed earlier, set up a problem-solving task that was designed to elicit principled mathematical knowledge. Further, she orchestrated a discussion around this task that encouraged students to support and critique their ideas. Talking about this lesson, Tory explained: "I think the students definitely have it solid now that if you're comparing two fractions, the size of the whole makes it or breaks it, as far as you have to compare fractions from the same whole. I think that they all know that the issue with the fourths and sixths is that it's not just the size of the piece but also the number of pieces. I think they're on the verge of that; I think probably half of the class really sees that." For Tory, having her students work on classroom tasks that engaged them with mathematical concepts was important.

In contrast, mathematical problem-solving in Isaro's classroom was mostly about procedural knowledge. Doing mathematics involved mostly remembering standard procedures and using these to calculate right answers. Problem solving did not involve any fundamental reconceptualization of what it meant to know mathematics nor was it an opportunity for students to reason about mathematical ideas.

Although there was evidence of "standards oriented" mathematics instruction in each of the twenty-five classrooms, instruction in most classrooms looked more like Isaro's than Tory's. Only four teachers were teaching mathematics in ways similar to Tory's instruction. In these four classrooms, the mathematical tasks that students worked on and their conversations about these tasks balanced principled and procedural mathematical knowledge. I label this Level 1 implementation because it most closely resembled the ideas pressed by the mathematics standards. I found Level 3 implementation in eleven of the twenty-five classrooms, including Isaro's. In these classrooms, both the tasks and discourse patterns remained firmly grounded in procedural mathematical knowledge. Level 2 implementation, found in ten of the twenty-five classrooms, fell somewhere between Tory's and Isaro's practices. We consider Level 1, 2, and 3 implementation patterns below.

Balancing Principled and Procedural Knowledge

Four teachers engaged students in tasks that centered on principled mathematical knowledge and that supported a conception of doing mathematics that involved more than computation. Mathematical tasks were designed to help students grasp mathematical concepts. Mathematics was not presented as a statement of end products—definitions, rules, procedures—for memorization and later regurgitation. For example, the task embedded in Tory's Jessie problem was designed to orient students to the idea that fractions are always a reference to a whole or unit. Another teacher, Marjie Yarrow, presented seventh-grade students with a task involving polygonal tessellation.* Students were asked to conjecture and test whether a range of irregular and regular polygons tessellate and if they did, to explain why they did. "They know how to make them but don't understand why certain polygons tessellate and why certain ones will not."

These teachers also set up mathematical tasks that represented

---

* Tessellation in mathematical terms is the covering of a geometric plane without gaps or overlaps using congruent plane figures of one or more types. In more common usage a tessellation is some sort of mosaic pattern using small squares of stone or glass. During the postlesson interview, Yarrow described the mathematical idea underlying the task: "There are patterns and relationships that occur in nature and in real life . . . There is a reason why people use certain shapes to tessellate and there are reasons why we use certain shapes to quilt and there are reasons why we use certain shapes to make a tile on the floor . . . And one of the reasons, one of the underlying math things is that it is 360 degrees around a point so that is why certain shapes work. You could have more than one shape to fit around a point. It doesn't have to be all triangles or all quadrilaterals, but the sum of their interior angles has to be 360."

doing mathematics as problem solving and exploring relations using various representations including concrete, pictorial, symbolic, and story-based. For example, the Jessie problem was not unlike a conventional story problem. What sets it apart, however, is that Tory set up the task so that students had to explain their thinking and answers using pictures and words. Simply deciding whether three-quarters and five-sixths were the same size was insufficient. Further, the tasks in these four classrooms were set up so that students could not solve the problems by applying mechanically some procedure. This contrasted sharply with the manner in which doing mathematics in school is typically presented as the statement of established mathematical truths (Romberg, 1983; Greeno, 1991).

Discourse patterns in these four classrooms also brought to the fore principled mathematical knowledge, providing students with opportunities to experience mathematics as more than computation. Teachers constantly pressed students to develop conjectures. They asked students to explain their reasoning and justify their solutions. As a result, students had opportunities to appreciate mathematics as involving devising and defending solutions to problems. Consider a representative exchange from Tory's classroom that took place just after Ron had drawn and explained his diagram, about twenty-five minutes into the mathematics lesson involving the Jessie problem described earlier:

ALEISHA (student): I think from the very beginning you probably got it wrong Ron. The five-sixths is a bigger whole than three-quarters.

TORY: What are you saying? You can go to the board.

JAY (student): His is too long. His whole rectangles need to be the same size.

ALEISHA: I agree. You have to keep them the same size.

TORY: Can you show us?

Aleisha went to the board and drew and shaded in three-quarters and five-sixths on the rectangles of equal size:

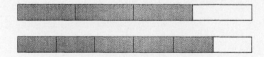

> TORY: Oh, Aleisha, you disagree with Ron for the same reason as Jay. Ron's rectangles needed to be the same size for a good proof.
>
> ALEISHA: Yes.
>
> TORY: What do we need to keep in mind here, class?
>
> STUDENTS: The bars [rectangles] should be equal.
>
> TORY: Can you say it differently?
>
> RYAN: The whole should be the same.
>
> TORY: This is important, can you see that Ron? They're saying that your model can't be used to compare the fractions.
>
> NATHAN (student): Ron, what did you do before?
>
> TORY: How many people made the mistake that your wholes were not equal? Would you change your mind now and think about the size of the whole? Can someone come up and represent this idea on a number line?

In this exchange, Tory continuously pressed students to explain and justify their answers with questions such as "Is this right, and if so, why do you agree?" "How do you know that?" "How does that make sense?" Simply having an answer, right or wrong, was insufficient. Students readily offered their opinions about their peers' ideas.

The situation was similar in the other three classrooms. For example, in Darla Land's fourth-grade classroom, students regularly asked classmates to defend or elaborate on their responses. She explained the importance of getting students to reason with each other: "Because they have to think in order to do that and I want them to think as often as possible during the day. So when they have to explain they have to go through this process of thinking how they arrived at their answer, and then also how am I going to explain it. And as they get better at it, the more they do it. So it is the thinking involved that I think is most important." Through their questions, these teachers helped students bring to the surface key mathematical concepts.

New Activities, Old Mathematics

Classroom tasks and discourse norms in the eleven classrooms in Level 3 implementation (including Isaro's) remained firmly grounded in procedural mathematical knowledge and computational skills. While we observed tasks that involved problem solving and applying mathematics to real-world situations, these tasks focused almost exclusively on procedural knowledge and facts. Moreover, these tasks represented mathematics as being chiefly, often exclusively, about computing right answers using predetermined formulas and procedures.

Isaro's Tuff's diner problem, detailed earlier, was representative of mathematical tasks in these eleven classrooms. There was potential for students to explore principled mathematical knowledge embedded in the Tuff's diner task. But Isaro presented the task as if it were exclusively about procedural knowledge by focusing students' attention on the long-division procedure. In fact, there were multiple ways that students might have approached solving the problem posed by Isaro, but her treatment of it as an opportunity to practice the long-division procedure suggested to students that there was only one right way. Problem solving was an occasion for students to practice applying procedures.

In another classroom, an eighth-grade middle-school mathematics teacher taught students a unit on the volume and surface area of pyramids, cones, and cylinders. On the blackboard was written the formula for finding the volume of a pyramid, $V =$

Bh/3. Following several examples, students solved a problem at their desks: "The pyramid in Egypt has a square base. Each side is 220 meters. The height is 137 meters. Find the volume." Students substituted the right numbers for each variable and completed the computations. The teacher's approach was identical for cones and cylinders. Tasks in other Level 3 implementation classrooms involved students solving numerous algebraic equations (for example, $x + 4 = 10$), answering one- or two-digit addition problems, plotting sixty pairs of positive and negative numbers on a "coordinate axis grid," and solving multidigit multiplication problems. Level 3 implementation teachers presented tasks in ways that focused students' attention on procedural knowledge and accurate computation.

The approach to problem solving that dominated Level 3 classrooms contrasts with that urged by the mathematics standards. From the perspective of the standards, real-world problems are distinctly different from traditional story problems in that solutions are not immediately obvious and they do not lend themselves to the wholesale application of ready-made procedures (NCTM, 1989). For all teachers in this third group, their tasks portrayed doing mathematics as a process of memorizing procedures and using these to calculate right answers by plugging in numbers. As one middle-school teacher articulated a frequently observed approach: "I want students to learn how to take a formula and replace it with values because they have been taught what the letters stand for . . . that's the only way students will understand it."

As one might expect, classroom discourse norms in these eleven classrooms reflected this focus on procedural knowledge. There was a push for right answers and an exclusive focus on procedural mathematical knowledge, whether students worked alone or in groups. Teachers asked almost all the questions, and students typically responded by articulating the procedures that led to an answer and / or the answer itself. Further discussion was rare. When students struggled with an answer, teachers waited for the correct response. They either turned to other students or provided the answer themselves.

Consider Isaro's classroom again. Having solved the Tuff's diner problem, she moved on to the next problem, forty-one divided by three, written on the overhead. Pointing to the overhead, Isaro said: "What are you going to be doing mentally? You ask yourself, will three go into four? Yes. So we'll have a number there and then you'll know three will go into the next number. The next step is that we have to divide into groups of three. We divided forty-one into three equal groups. Three goes into forty-one. Now we have three equal groups and there is one ten in each group and one ten left." She proceeded to solve the problem at the board using long division. She asked students at the overhead to regroup using the paper clips (the paper clips are placed on top of the overhead, which is turned off). Once students had finished regrouping, Isaro asked: "What do we have left?" Students responded in chorus, "Remainder." At that point, Isaro went through the procedures to solve the problem: "The first step is to divide, then multiply. The third step is, what do you do? You subtract. The fourth step is to compare answers . . . Divide, multiply, subtract, compare, bring down, last one start over." After a few practice problems, students worked on a series of two- and three-digit long-division problems at their desks for the remainder of the lesson.

It was not unusual for students in Level 3 classrooms to work together in small groups on problems, and to use manipulatives and calculators. In this respect, the instruction they experienced overlapped with the mathematics standards. But what counted as mathematics and doing mathematics was firmly grounded in procedural knowledge and computing right answers.

Principled Tasks, Procedural Discourse
Mathematics instruction in the remaining ten classrooms fell somewhere between Tory's and Isaro's approaches. The academic

tasks in these classrooms were oriented toward principled mathematical knowledge. But the conversations around these tasks focused chiefly on procedural mathematical knowledge.

These ten teachers set up tasks that required students to work through problem situations in order to explore and discover mathematical concepts and relations. Doing mathematics was represented in these tasks as a process of exploring relations, typically using concrete, pictorial, and symbolic representations. One elementary teacher, Karen Bedford, for example, had students investigate the relations among fractions (that is, halves, thirds, and sixths) using concrete, pictorial, and symbolic representations of the fractions. She explained that a goal of this unit on equivalent fractions involved helping students grasp that the whole could be divided in a variety of ways (for example, two halves, or one third and four sixths). The task asked students to find all possible combinations for dividing up a hexagon cookie using three shapes—triangles (representing sixths), red trapezoids (representing halves), and green rhombuses (representing thirds).* Using flat hexagon (yellow), triangle (blue), trapezoid (red), and rhombus (green) "cookies," students explored different ways of dividing up the unit (represented by the hexagon). They recorded the combinations they discovered by filling out blank hexagons on their worksheet.

Although these teachers presented tasks that were grounded in principled knowledge, the questions the teacher posed during the enactment of these tasks focused students on procedural knowledge. They failed to make the principled knowledge public. These ten teachers typically asked questions that required students to do little more than supply the right answer. Consider an example of the conversation that ensued in Bedford's classroom during the lesson on equivalent fractions just described.

---

* Students were not told that the various shapes represented different fractions—one-half, one-third, or one-sixth—that information began to emerge only toward the end of the lesson.

Bedford reviewed the activity with students, immediately drawing their attention to the first and second hexagon cookies on the overhead (the overhead included all possible combinations as defined by the teacher):

BEDFORD: How many blues (pointing to the first hexagon cookies)?

STUDENTS: Two.

BEDFORD: Wait now, raise your hands to answer. How many greens? (Four hands up.) Jon? (One of the four who had volunteered an answer.)

JON: Two.

BEDFORD: Right. So what's the combination here? (Five hands go up.) Amanda?

AMY (student): Two blue, two green.

BEDFORD: Right. [Moving on to the next hexagon cookie.] How many greens, Alex?

ALEX: Two.

BEDFORD: Right, how many blues?

The teacher worked through all eight combinations in this fashion, stopping occasionally to allow students to check that they had the correct combination.

Bedford fundamentally transformed the mathematical task by virtue of the way she engaged students in talking about the work. All that was required of students in Bedford's classroom during the whole-group discussion was to count the number of reds, or greens, or blues in the teacher's representations on the overhead. Her questions were designed to elicit the one right answer from students. For example, the manner in which Bedford presented students with a completed overhead, the finished product, shut out opportunities for students to reason about the legitimacy of the combinations they had discovered. Teachers in the second group infrequently attempted, and rarely managed, to bring to the surface students' mathematical thinking.

Students in these ten classrooms were rarely pushed to elaborate on their answers, let alone justify them. If students' responses did not reflect the correct answer, teachers did not raise follow-up questions to make students' mathematical thinking explicit. If students' responses did reflect the correct answer, teachers paraphrased the answer, changing it slightly to make it more "accurate." For example, during a lesson on 3-D shapes in one third-grade classroom, the teacher asked students for examples of a hemisphere. One student, Jake, offered "an upside-down bowl." The teacher replied, "an upside-down bowl, if you turn it over and the rounded part is on top" and moved quickly to ask another student, Sandy, for her answers. Sandy offered, "a helmet and an upside-down bowl," to which the teacher responded, "a helmet, that's a good idea" before calling on another student. The teacher did not ask students to explain why a "helmet" or an "upside-down bowl" were hemispheres. Such a discussion might have helped both teacher and students appreciate that most bowls, right-side-up or upside-down, differ from helmets and are not perfectly hemispherical. Further, students were never given opportunities to present their conjectures and were not encouraged to do so. Consequently, opportunities to understand the underlying principled mathematical knowledge embedded in the tasks were curtailed.

Students' opportunities to appreciate doing mathematics were also limited by these discourse patterns. If students are to appreciate what it means to do mathematics, they will need opportunities to make and revise conjectures, to reason with one another about their mathematical ideas, and to justify their solutions and methods to others (Lampert, 1990; Lakatos, 1986; NCTM, 1989). While students in these classrooms did talk with one another about mathematics, there were no sustained arguments about mathematical concepts or conversations on the merits of a particular process or solution. Their discourse focused instead on getting the right answer.

Teachers nonetheless seemed to recognize the importance of having students publicly explain and support their ideas. For example, Bedford argued that getting students to talk about mathematics was key: "I think it's important that we can get students to talk and verbalize what's in their heads." All ten teachers believed that communicating about mathematics was important because it pressed students to think through the mathematics. Yet we found scant evidence that these teachers encouraged students to explain or justify their mathematical thinking. They were aware that engaging students in conversations about mathematics was important, but acknowledged that nurturing these conversations was difficult. One elementary teacher remarked, "As a teacher, I find it really hard not to give them the answer." Other teachers made similar comments.

My analysis suggests that the mathematics standards have progressed slowly and erratically in classroom practice. Clearly, however, some teachers can and do practice in ways that resonate with the mathematics standards. These teachers' instructional practices are evidence that fundamentally reforming mathematics practice is possible; they offer a sort of existence proof that the standards can be implemented in real classrooms.

How did some teachers manage to set up classroom tasks that focused students' attention on principled mathematical knowledge while others did not?

Teachers' Opportunities for Sense-Making

Teachers' attention to the standards was one plausible explanation for the uneven progress of standards among classrooms. But all teachers reported giving extraordinary attention to the mathematics standards. They all claimed that they were "fairly" or "very" familiar with either the state's "Essential Goals and Objectives for Mathematics Education" or the MEAP for mathematics. Indeed, twenty-one teachers reported being either "fairly" or "very" familiar with the NCTM standards. The standards had definitely captured teachers' attention.

Another possible explanation concerned teachers' willingness to go along with the advice offered by the standards. But again, all twenty-five teachers were willing to revise their instruction in ways that they understood to be consistent with the standards. None were resisting the standards. In fact, they expressed strong agreement with the ideas they understood from the standards. All twenty-five teachers claimed that it was "very important" for students to "understand how math is used in the real world." Twenty-four teachers reported that it was "very important" for students to understand math concepts, principles, and strategies" if they were to be good in math at school; one reported that it was "somewhat" important. These teachers were keen to revise their teaching in order to incorporate the ideas they understood from the standards.

Another explanation concerns teachers' prior practice; perhaps the four teachers who taught mathematics instruction in ways that most closely resonated with the standards had always taught in this way or done so for some time. If this were the case, these teachers would have had to make only minor changes to their existing practice. Yarrow's case lends support to this explanation. A latecomer to teaching, Yarrow encountered the mathematics standards and ideas about their entailments for teaching through her teacher preparation program. But this was not the case for the other three teachers who managed to teach in ways that were most closely aligned with the standards. These three were all veteran teachers with between nine and eighteen years' teaching experience, and all reported teaching mathematics in very conventional ways into the late 1980s. One remarked about her prior practice: "It was more like practicing algorithms and writing them out of the book." Teachers' prior practice did not provide a satisfactory explanation for the uneven progress of standards in classrooms.

Another explanation concerns teachers' prior knowledge; teachers who were more knowledgeable could be more likely to appreciate the deeper changes pressed by the standards and implement them more faithfully. Again, this explanation was unsatisfactory. For example, Tory did not bring to the standards any special interest in mathematics or extensive mathematical knowledge. She remarked, "I was not a good math student myself . . . and I'm as bad off as I think a lot of elementary teachers are who are not strong math people." Two of the four teachers claimed they were not especially interested in or knowledgeable about mathematics. Only one of the teachers who managed a Level 1 implementation had a background in mathematics.

Finally, the curricular materials that teachers used failed to account for differences in their implementation of the standards. Some teachers were using curricula that were consistent with the standards. For example, two of the four teachers whose practice most closely approximated the standards were using a mathematics curriculum that was designed to support the NCTM standards. But some of those teachers whose practice only modestly or weakly aligned with the standards were using the same curriculum.

Teachers' Sense-Making about Standards and Practice

Just like district policymakers, teachers had to make sense of the standards. They had to work out what the standards—as represented in state and district policies and other sources of advice— meant. They had to figure out what these ideas entailed for their teaching and grapple with getting them to work in their classrooms. Trying out their understandings in practice by taking the reform ideas for a test run, they had to learn to get past the failures and tweak the practices or even redesign them entirely. There was much that teachers had to work out in order to get the reform ideas to succeed in their classrooms because state and district policies had not provided teachers with scripts or blueprints for their work. Even if they had, there would still be much for teachers to figure out.

Moreover, as teachers put these reform ideas into practice, they encountered various challenges. For example, Howard struggled with figuring out at what point she ought to provide struggling students with a resolution to a mathematics problem. She explained: "I thought it maybe would be useful for the students to struggle with this and I think for some of the kids, this made sense . . . even though it was difficult to think about . . . I was constantly debating in my mind should we cut this conversation off or should I let it go and see what they can come up with." Other teachers spoke about the difficulty of nurturing more open-ended conversations during mathematics lessons while trying not to give students the answers.

To understand the full import of the mathematics standards, teachers would have had to fundamentally change their scripts for mathematics and mathematics instruction. Many teachers like Isaro understood, unwittingly, the standards to involve relatively modest changes in their existing mental scripts and practice. Isaro was convinced that she was following the standards even though her teaching remained firmly focused on procedural mathematical knowledge. Developing new understandings of familiar ideas such as problem solving was very difficult because it entailed discrediting and abandoning deeply held scripts for mathematics and developing alternative ones.

Still, Tory managed to make such changes in her teaching and practice. And she encountered the standards having personal expertise in neither mathematics nor mathematics education. While expertise was important in teachers' efforts to make sense of the standards, it was not the only thing that differentiated opportunities for sense-making from one teacher to the next. Specifically, the ways in which teachers figured out the ideas pressed by standards and worked out the entailments of these ideas for their practice differed from one teacher to the next. Isaro's opportunities to notice, make sense of, and check out emerging understandings, and figure out what these meant for classroom practice, were distinctly different from those of Tory.

Sense-Making as a Social or Solo Endeavor. Those four teachers whose practice most closely resembled the standards described their efforts to make sense of standards as a social endeavor. For these teachers, especially the three veteran Riverville teachers, sustained conversations with colleagues were central in their efforts to understand the ideas pushed by the standards and figure out how to get these ideas into practice. Social resources, including social networks and trust, were critical to these teachers' sense-making. The job of figuring out what the standards meant was shared or distributed for the three Riverville teachers; they did not have to go it alone. Trying out new ideas in their classrooms, with the continual support of colleagues to help iron out implementation problems, increased the likelihood that these teachers would stay the course and not abandon their efforts to implement the standards.

These conversations enabled teachers to develop deeper understandings of central reform ideas. Howard explained that when she first heard about the importance of discourse in mathematics, she and some of her colleagues were not entirely sure what it meant: "We were reading and hearing about classroom discourse, but we didn't quite know what it meant at that point." After getting together to talk about the role of discourse with other teachers, however, she developed a better understanding of the importance of discourse in mathematics: "Part of what has been so important has been our discussion. We have a professional group of people who are willing to get together and talk about ideas and share ideas and talk about failure and successes so we can help each other grow. That's been really helpful." These discussions allowed teachers to exchange ideas and check out their emerging understandings of ideas such as mathematical problem solving and discourse. Howard attributed changes in her mathematics teaching in important part to deliberations with colleagues.

For the three Riverville teachers, deliberations with colleagues were both formal and informal. The school district created a variety of formal opportunities for teachers to work together on the standards, including summer professional development workshops. These formal opportunities were supplemented by brief but ongoing lunchtime and hallway conversations. Advice from experts from inside and outside the district enhanced these ongoing deliberations about the standards.

Social networks also created incentives for teachers to revise their practice. Teachers developed a sense of obligation to each other to improve their practice in rather particular ways, as a result of their ongoing conversations with colleagues. Their classrooms became less private as other teachers and outside experts observed and discussed their practice. One teacher remarked: "Mandy was just dragging us along. She dragged Kathy and got her involved, and Kathy dragged Charlene, and now we're all dragging others. I guess because it was a teacher-initiated kind of thing teachers are willing to get involved in it."

The fourth teacher, Yarrow, was relatively new to teaching. Her preservice education had equipped her with the expertise to teach in ways consistent with the standards. But she reached beyond her local school district to build a social network to support her efforts to better understand and implement the standards. Yarrow's colleagues in rural Littleton were not interested in working with her to better understand what the mathematics standards entailed for instruction. Still, she persisted. Encouraged and equipped by her preservice education, Yarrow sought out opportunities to learn outside of her district. She noted, "I am pulling things from NCTM conferences, just talking with other people. I belong to a learning community group through the math science center in Sun City. So I am just trying to pull all these resources together and come up with a great program that will help kids learn and motivate them."

The other twenty-one teachers described their sense-making efforts as more solitary experiences. Of course none of these teachers were recluses; their engagement with the standards did involve contact with others whether through attendance at a professional development workshop or a hallway exchange. Still, for these twenty-one teachers much of the work of figuring out the mathematics standards was done without others. They attended workshops and took courses, but were for the most part left on their own to grapple with what the standards involved for their teaching once they returned to their classrooms. Talking about their opportunities to learn, only six of these teachers referred to having conversations with colleagues about mathematics instruction. A suburban elementary teacher noted, "There isn't a daily 'How do you teach this?' Or 'What did you do for this?' That kind of interaction doesn't happen."

Only three of these teachers engaged in any sustained, regular conversations about mathematics instruction. Instead, their conversations were impromptu and mostly involved the exchange of activities for students to work on or topics to cover. One teacher said, "Because the MEAP was so important to my colleague at that time, she was telling me some of the things that they needed to know for the MEAP." Another remarked about a workshop she attended: "Mostly it was listening. Attending sessions and listening." These teachers never described conversations in which they worked to figure out some instructional ideas pressed by the standards. Hence, these teachers had few opportunities to test out their understandings of these ideas. In such circumstances, it was easy for teachers like Isaro to convince themselves that their teaching resonated with the standards.

Coherence and Focus in Teachers' Opportunities for Sense-Making. Teachers' opportunities to make sense of the standards also differed in the extent to which they cohered around the standards for mathematics education. Those teachers whose practice most closely approximated the standards had sense-making opportunities that cohered around and were firmly grounded in the standards. For Yarrow, this coherence was achieved through her teacher preparation program and the social networks she maintained beyond the Littleton school district.

For the three Riverville teachers, the coherence and focus of their sense-making opportunities were a function of their school district's initiatives around the standards. Coherence was achieved in part by grounding deliberations about practice in the curricular materials that teachers were using in their classrooms; materials that were consistent with the standards. Teachers reported using a variety of curricular materials, the NCTM standards, and videotapes by Marilyn Burns, a curriculum expert, to focus their conversations about the mathematics reforms. One teacher described how these materials facilitated their discussions about mathematics practice: "We tried to study the NCTM standards and go to presentations about them. We've looked at Marilyn Burns's tapes, we've looked at Deborah Ball [a national expert on mathematics education] . . . and a couple of our people here have taken coursework about math, and so we try to share all that information." A new middle-school mathematics curriculum and the adoption of Investigations Math in all elementary grades focused teachers' conversations about mathematics instruction by providing common points of reference.

In contrast, most other teachers' opportunities to learn were not always even directly related to mathematics instruction. They reported attending university courses and workshops, typically one or two, on "mastery learning," "multiple intelligencies," "manipulatives," "problem solving," "multiplying fractions," "the Michigan Educational Assessment Program," "geometry," "cooperative grouping," "outcome-based education," "using computers in instruction," "alternative assessment," "using different mathematical representations to teach mathematics," and "cooperative learning." The workshops described by these teachers addressed either some discrete aspect of mathematics education or some subject-matter-neutral topic. Six of the twenty-one teachers reported that their learning opportunities were not specific to mathematics.

These twenty-one teachers also reported that their occasions to learn from and about the standards were frequently brief "awareness sessions." One teacher noted with respect to monthly meetings about mathematics: "The district officials just bring ideas and say 'Well here, maybe you want to try this.'" Another teacher made a similar observation: "People come sometimes from downtown and talk in the morning . . . and there were inservices during the day at school. Most of the ones that I attended were by the math specialist and just kind of gave us some suggestions about how we could improve our teaching so that the children would do better on the MEAP." Yet another teacher remarked:

> Well, the district had grade-level meetings . . . And since we all couldn't go to all of them I had probability and statistics that I had a half-day on. And all they did was go over those different areas that need to be taught in probability and statistics. I went to one other one . . . it might have been numeration. This was when the new MEAP test was given and they wanted us to be aware of all the components of that test and what we would have to teach to build up to that. But that was a half-day. It wasn't teaching strategies. It was the type of material the children would have to know. They did give us a folder of activities that we could do with them.

External experts gave teachers information in brief workshops and the teachers were then encouraged to put this information into practice in their classrooms. It was left up to the teachers to work the information they got at these workshops and courses into some coherent vision for instruction.

Going Public with Classroom Practice. For those teachers whose practice most closely resembled the standards, their sense-making opportunities were firmly grounded in their efforts to put the mathematics standards into practice. While all teachers viewed their daily teaching and their students as important influences on their attempts to revise their instructional practice, only the three Riverville teachers described their efforts to make sense of standards as grounded in "public" discussions of their classroom practice. These teachers described ongoing conversations with colleagues that addressed their day-to-day attempts to implement the standards as pivotal in accounting for the substantial changes they had managed in their teaching over the past few years. Teachers' ongoing deliberations were simultaneously grounded both in the standards and in their efforts to implement the ideas they understood from the standards. One teacher remarked: "I think some of it is me watching other teachers. I've been to a couple of workshop situations and we sit around and watch a teacher teach a class so that we can see a different idea of what is going on and have conversations after either watching them on videotape or watching live sometimes . . . we sit down as a staff and talk about different ideas." Another teacher remarked: "I did some observing. The teacher that used to be in this building, we taught the same grade, but she was a major math person. So when she would try something in there, we'd kind of do it together or I'd come in and watch her do it or at least we'd sit at lunch and talk about well wow, this happened in my math class today. What happened with your lesson? And we'd kind of talk and plan together and talk about readjusting things." Conversations that were grounded in classroom observations and in teachers' attempts to put the standards into practice allowed these teachers to develop a deeper understanding of the ideas pressed by the standards. Further, these conversations enabled these teachers to appreciate what the mathematics standards entailed for their teaching and to develop the practical knowledge necessary for teaching in that way. Even when these three Riverville teachers' sense-making opportunities were outside the school district, classroom instruction was central.

The three Riverville teachers apprehended the reforms in an environment that supported ongoing inquiry about the standards and what they meant for classroom practice. They had replaced the norm of privacy, standard operating procedure in most schools, with a norm of deliberating openly about their practice with fellow teachers who were attempting to implement the standards as well as local and external experts. These deliberations focused simultaneously on understanding the standards and on teachers' efforts to implement the standards in their practice. Further, curriculum materials that embodied the reform ideas lent focus and coherence to teachers' deliberations.

With two exceptions (two teachers from the Riverville school district), the other twenty-one teachers never mentioned deliberations with colleagues about classroom practice as an important resource for making sense of the standards. All spoke about their practice and students as key influences on their practice, but their practice was mainly private and rarely deliberated about with colleagues. Mostly, they understood their opportunities to make sense of the mathematics standards as something that took place outside their classrooms in formal workshops and university courses.

Teacher Sense-Making and Organizational Arrangements

Teachers' sense-making opportunities were not a function of chance. Some teachers by virtue of the school districts and schools they worked in had access to tremendous social resources. The three Riverville teachers whose practice most closely approximated the standards understood the standards and worked out what they entailed for day-to-day teaching with considerable support from others.

The Riverville school district was instrumental in creating these rich sense-making opportunities. Riverville's curriculum director remarked: "We talk about the actual materials and the teaching techniques . . . We do a lot of talking about the NCTM standards and the research and try to integrate all of those things." She went on to explain: "It all goes back to the culture . . . As a classroom teacher when my door is closed, I do what I wanna do. And that's the culture we're trying to change. We are a community of learners."

A school administrator described a similar push for Riverville teachers to observe and discuss each others' teaching: "If the teachers want to go see somebody or watch somebody or take the day off to meet with another teacher to discuss an issue, that's very easily done. We'll work that out . . . The change comes from that teacher getting the idea, finding the time to sit down and organize that idea, and making it happen." These administrators viewed conversations among teachers as opportunities for them to grapple with the meaning of reform proposals and to develop an appreciation for what these proposals entailed for classroom practice. They worked to create these sense-making opportunities.

Others, indeed most teachers, were less fortunate. They worked in school districts where the social resources were scarce or at least district policymakers never mobilized them to support teachers' efforts to figure out the standards. Teachers in these districts had, for the most part, to go it alone.

These differences between districts were consequential when it came to teachers' implementation of the mathematics standards. As discussed in Chapters 3 and 4, Riverville, along with suburban Pleasant Valley and Parkwood, developed policies that endorsed a transformation of what counted as mathematical knowledge and doing mathematics. But Riverville differed from the two suburban districts in one important respect: Riverville's policymakers worked to create opportunities for teacher sense-making that were social, coherent, and grounded in ongoing conversations about teachers' practice. As shown in Table 7.1, three of the five

Table 7.1 Classroom implementation by district policy support for standards and district approach to teacher learning

Level of classroom implementation	Low-support, individualistic approach	High-support, individualistic approach	High-support, social approach
Level 1	1	0	3
Level 2	4	4	2
Level 3	5	6	0

Riverville teachers' practices closely approximated the standards. The other two Riverville teachers' practices were not as closely aligned with the standards; while their academic tasks were oriented to principled mathematical knowledge, the discourse around these tasks focused chiefly on procedural mathematical knowledge. Of the remaining twenty teachers, ten worked in either suburban Pleasant Valley or Parkwood, where district policies provided strong support for the standards but failed to create opportunities for teacher sense-making that cohered around the standards and were grounded in ongoing teacher deliberations about their mathematics instruction.

The extent to which the school district's policies support the mathematics standards influenced classroom-level implementation. Further, classroom implementation also depended on the opportunities that school-district policymakers created for teacher sense-making from and about the standards. The school district, however, did not have a monopoly on teacher sense-making. Though not a focus of the current study, teachers' accounts suggest that a school's culture influenced their opportunities for sense-making from and about the standards.

Of course, school districts can't make sense of standards for teachers or cause them to interpret the standards one way rather than another. Take the five Riverville teachers. Two of them made sense of the standards and taught mathematics in ways that were not nearly as closely aligned with the mathematics standards as the methods their three colleagues used. Yet these two teachers worked in Riverville, where district policies provided strong support for the standards and where district policies created rich opportunities for teachers' sense-making. Indeed, one of these teachers worked in the same school as Tory. Because teachers' sense-making opportunities were also a function of their knowledge and experiences, the school district influenced teachers' sense-making but did not determine its nature or outcome.

Yarrow's case offers further evidence that school districts' influence was not everything when it came to teacher sense-making. She worked in a district with relatively few social resources to support teacher sense-making from and about the mathematics standards. Yet she managed to forge her own social resources. Reaching beyond her school and school district, she used professional associations and contacts developed during her preservice education to establish networks that supported her efforts to implement the standards. Yarrow's determination, coupled with her expertise in mathematics education, enabled her to forge her own social network when her school district failed to deliver.

Relations between district policies and teachers' implementation of the standards were mediated by a variety of other variables. A regression equation to predict classroom implementation of the mathematics standards would include variables for "school," "district," and "teachers' knowledge and experiences" (among others), with the value of any one variable in predicting classroom implementation depending in some measure on the other variables. In all of this mix, the school district matters when it comes to the classroom implementation of state and national standards. The extent to which it matters and how it matters, however, depends in part on the other variables.

CHAPTER 8

Implementation Reconsidered

Roadblocks to successful implementation of policy are often portrayed as a function of the shirking and slacking of district policymakers, school leaders, and teachers. My account suggests otherwise. Sonny Naughton was neither dawdling nor dragging his feet when it came to the mathematics and science standards. He was certainly not resisting these efforts to reform mathematics and science education. On the contrary, school-district policymakers and schoolteachers were working hard to support the standards and figure out how to work their interpretations of these ideas into their daily practice. They were intent on implementing state and national standards.

Yet good intentions only go so far. When it comes to implementing new ideas about instruction, all the will in the world is not enough. In analyzing the standards as they seeped into local school districts and classrooms, what mattered most was what district leaders and teachers came to understand about their practice from the standards. Putting human sense-making center

stage in the implementation process illuminates how district policymakers and teachers construct messages about changing their
practice from policies that often misconstrue the intention of
policymakers. When locals understand ideas about revising their
practice from policies that are inconsistent with or fall short of
those intended by the policymakers, they unwittingly and un-
knowingly undermine the local implementation of these policies.
Misunderstandings or partial understandings of ideas are commonplace, and not confined to school districts and schools. They
are part and parcel of everyday life. We rarely have time to check
out our understanding of every new idea we hear; we live, often
unaware, with incomplete understandings or misunderstandings.
This is as likely to happen in congressional offices or the ivory
towers of academia as it is in school-district offices and schools.

As policy moves from the statehouse to the schoolhouse,
school districts work to figure out what the policy entails for their
work. School-district officials make their sense of the policy and
pass their understandings on to school leaders and teachers, who
of course may have already developed their own understandings
of the new policy. Private consultants, professional development
providers, professional associations, and others outside the formal school system also develop their own understandings of the
policy. Through workshops, consultations, and other means, they
pass these along to school personnel.

As I suggested in Chapter 1, the implementation process is
analogous to the telephone game. State policymakers and national reformers relay new ideas about instruction to the field
writ large. District policymakers construct understandings of
these ideas and pass their understandings on to school leaders
and teachers. But district policymakers frequently draw on multiple lines of communication—professional associations, other
states' policies, national standards—to inform their ideas about
instructional policy. As the preceding chapters document, however, district policymakers' understandings often miss or miscon-

strue elements of the policy message. Of course, school leaders and teachers encounter takes on the policy message not only from district policymakers and state documents but also from a variety of others—private consultants, professional associations, and academics—who make their sense of state policy and communicate it to school districts and schools.

But the telephone-game metaphor only goes so far. In real life, things are seldom as simple as they are in games, though games have an uncanny way of capturing experience. First, state policy rarely has a direct connection to the school district, school, or classroom. Multiple lines of communication relay renditions of the policy to school districts and schools. In some respects, it is like a party line with numerous accounts of the reform ideas being relayed at once. In other ways, implementation is like multiple crisscrossing lines relaying reform ideas to school districts and schools. Conversations overlap and parallel one another. Moreover, in real life the players rarely if ever get to stand back and see how the story evolved in its telling and retelling.

Interactive Policymaking

School districts are key players between the statehouse and the schoolhouse, and in their policymaking stance on instructional issues, they do not function chiefly as the implementation arm of state or federal agencies. Ann Smith made policy about science education for Lakeside public schools. Like policymakers elsewhere in the school system, she convened a committee of teachers and administrators and she drew from numerous sources to inform the policy writing process. She also received local school board approval for the science curriculum, developed an implementation plan, and raised foundation money to support the plan. The situation was similar for Sonny Naughton in Littleton.

Policymaking in education is not a zero-sum game; school-district policymaking expands in tandem with state and federal policy initiatives. As documented in the preceding chapters, state and national standards enabled rather than constrained district-level policymaking about mathematics and science education. State and national standards featured more prominently in some district policymaking efforts than others. While the state policy was center stage in Sonny Naughton's efforts in Littleton, for example, it was only one of the many sources that informed Ann Smith's efforts at Lakeside.

School-district policymaking mattered for state and national standards. Some districts made policies that supported the standards. Most districts made policies that supported some aspects of the standards but failed to support others. When districts made policies that supported some of the instructional ideas pressed by standards but not others, they limited the opportunities that teachers in their school districts had to understand and implement the standards. In this way, district policymaking limits the classroom effects of state or federal policies.

The interactive policymaking view underscores that the local implementation of state and federal policies depends on how they are supported by school-district policies. If state or federal policies are to influence what school districts do, they will have to do so through the district policymaking process. Because federal agencies and most state governments lack the infrastructure to guide classroom instruction in hundreds of thousands of far-flung classrooms, they depend on school districts for the successful implementation of their policies at the school level. Recent state budget deficits will likely further erode the capacity of state departments of education, increasing reliance on school districts.

What Is *the* Policy?

One issue in all of this concerns whether writing about *the* policy is something of a misnomer. The state's mathematics and science policies consisted of a number of instruments, each of which represented "the policy." The policy came in a variety of shapes and sizes—the state's assessment system, the standards documents, other state department publications, and presentations by state officials. Moreover, these instruments became interweaved with national standards for mathematics and science education as they found their way to local school districts. One might refer to these renditions as the policy. But these renditions did not replicate one another. They were different representations of a set of ideas about reforming mathematics and science education. For example, the state's mathematics assessment instrument, in the eyes of some state policymakers, did a poor job of representing some of the core ideas about mathematics content and pedagogy pressed by the state's objectives. Which was the policy? We might say that both were "the policy," but their inconsistency makes that problematic. Of course, consistency is partly in the eye of the beholder. For classroom teachers, the state assessment instrument was a more potent representation of the policy, especially in science, than were the state's goals and objectives.

These matters get even more complicated at the local level. As just noted, school districts do not treat state policy as a hand-me-down to schools; they make their own policies. By virtue of the policies they develop on curriculum guidelines, curricular materials, and staff development, school districts are key instructional policymakers. Occupying an influential mediating position between state (and federal) agencies and the schoolhouse, school districts send teachers messages about instruction that sometimes amplify and sometimes misrepresent, unintentionally, the ideas promoted by state and national standards. Because most teachers relied on school-district policy, it became the state policy for them. As I documented in earlier chapters, school districts were not of one mind about revising mathematics and science education, so teachers received rather different advice about doing "the policy" depending on their school district. This suggests that policy might best be thought about as plural rather than singular.

What Is Policy Success?

Policy analysts always want to know whether a policy worked or not. Questions about policy effects, however, rarely involve yes or no answers. My account suggests that the mathematics and science standards were not a huge success, but they were not a total flop either.

If the core intent of the mathematics and science standards was to fundamentally transform what students learn and how they learn, then Michigan's policy initiatives were not a success. The limited influence of the standards on what counted as mathematics and science content and doing these subjects in classrooms is sobering. It is of special concern because what gets taught, especially as reflected in academic tasks and discourse norms, is a critical influence on student learning and achievement. This is further evidence that policy is a rather crude instrument, perhaps ill-suited to forging fundamental change in instruction. Considering the significant attention that state policy received from district policymakers and teachers, these results are all the more surprising.

The preceding chapters, however, also offer some cause for optimism. Implementation research is replete with doom-and-gloom accounts of policy rarely getting beyond the classroom door. Policy and classroom instruction are typically portrayed as disconnected from one another. But district policymakers and teachers in my study were not turning a blind eye to state policymakers' proposals. They heeded policy and teachers worked hard to put their understandings of the policy into practice in their classrooms. The mathematics and science standards did reach into schools and beyond the classroom door. Teachers took seriously state policy as mediated by school-district policies.

Still, the standards had more influence on some aspects of teachers' instruction than others. Instruction is a multidimensional practice. Classroom instruction includes, among other things, the questions teachers pose to students, the materials students and teachers work with, the ways students interact with each other and the teacher, and academic tasks. My account suggests that policy penetrated some aspects of teachers' instructional practices more easily than others. On some dimensions instructional practice looked very similar across classrooms and was consistent with ideas pressed by the standards. For example, in most mathematics classrooms teachers taught problem solving, linked mathematics to the real world, used multiple representations and concrete materials, and used a combination of whole-class, small-group, and individual instruction. Concerning what counted as mathematical knowledge and doing inquiry in mathematics, however, instruction varied considerably among classrooms, with only a handful of teachers practicing in ways aligned with the standards. Thus some core dimensions of classroom practice such as the academic task and discourse norms appear to be especially resilient.

It is important to remember, however, that some veteran teachers like Tory did manage to fundamentally change their instruction on these dimensions in response to the standards. None of these teachers was very knowledgeable about mathematics and they had no particular interest in the subject. Moreover, the ideas were new to these teachers; they would not have encountered them in their professional preparation. Yet they revised their mathematics teaching in ways that were relatively consistent with the standards. These teachers are proof that policy, under the right conditions, can enable teachers to make fundamental changes to their practice. One reason then why single or dichotomous measures of the implementation of instructional policy are rarely possible is because teaching is not monolithic—it is a complex, multifaceted practice.

Another reason that pronouncements about the success of a policy are complicated is that scholars are not in agreement about what constitutes success. Academic deliberations are often polarized around either the perspective of the local implementer—the district administrator or classroom teacher—or that of the policymaker (Lipsky, 1980; Linder and Peters, 1987). From the implementers' view, dubbed the bottom-up perspective, policy might be deemed a success if it fit with implementers' agendas, roles, and needs. In contrast, from the more conventional top-down perspective, policy is thought to be a success if implementers comply and follow the rules and regulations generating the outcomes sought by the policy (Van Meter and Van Horn, 1975). If I had relied entirely on the view from the bottom—the implementers' perspective—I might have concluded that the policy was a success. After all, for the most part it fit with the agendas and interests of district policymakers and teachers. If I had taken an exclusively top-down perspective, I might have concluded that the policy was a flop.

I argue that both the top-down and bottom-up perspectives need to be used together in order to access the success of a policy. Efforts to gauge the success of policy from the top down dwell exclusively on evidence of standards in practice, but fail to take account of how far school districts and schools have moved or have to move in response to the policy. Analysts working from the bottom up often forget about policy goals and present descriptive accounts of how things are as prescriptions for how things ought to be. What should be done often becomes what can be done.

Combining the two perspectives means that both state and national reformers' goals as well as where local policymakers and teachers are coming from are critical in making any determinations about the success of a policy. Looking only from the top down, those school districts that developed local policies for the first time but whose policies neglected to support core aspects of the standards might be deemed evidence of the failure of state and national standards. But when one considers that these school districts never before had policies that specified what students should learn in mathematics and science education, they represent something of a success for state and national standards. Similarly, Karen Bedford's mathematics teaching with the classroom discourse grounded in procedural knowledge suggests limited success when viewed from the perspective of state and national standards. When the same mathematics teaching is viewed from the perspective of her teaching five years earlier, however, it suggests something of a success for state policy. Progress has as much to do with where one started out as with one's proximity to some destination.

Policy, People, and Place

People play a prominent role in my account. Accounts that foreground the individual in the implementation have become more and more popular in education and, in many cases, continue to generate rich insights into the policy implementation process. These attempts to factor the person and agency into the implementation process, however, have at times pushed the pendulum so far as to understate the role of the situation—organizational structure, political circumstances, and the like. If I had focused only on individual teachers, for example, and ignored the organizations in which they practiced, I might easily, and mistakenly, have accounted for teachers' responses to the standards in terms of their individual differences; that is, differences in their prior knowledge and experience. In the process, I would have missed distinctions that were associated with their situation. Teachers' and district policymakers' actions do not take place in a vacuum but in a complex web of organizational structures and traditions. While the knowledge and experience of individuals matter in terms of what sense they make of policy, the organizational circumstances in which they make sense also matter. Moreover, they matter in interaction.

To account for implementation failure, some scholars have built explanatory models that connect individual and organizational factors. The uncertainty regarding means and ends of teaching and other street-level work, the unpredictability of worker-client relations, and the difficulty of supervising the work contribute to policy having limited influence on practice (Lipsky, 1980). According to this view, structurally or organizationally determined roles shape what teachers do with respect to policy. Although individuals loom large in Lipsky's account, social and organizational circumstances determine their practice with respect to policy. The model thus fails to account for the sorts of variation among teachers and district policymakers documented in earlier chapters.

Individuals figure prominently in my account, but the organizational circumstances of their work do also. Social structure or organizational circumstances are not all determining; teachers and district policymakers do exercise agency. A "person-centered" approach to policy analysis (Lewis and Maruna, 1998) makes good sense, but in foregrounding the person it is important not to lose sight of place, where the person is positioned. The cognitive perspective on implementation I have developed in this book merges human agency and social structure. Social organization shapes what people do and is also shaped by peoples' actions. In this way, organizational structure is both the medium of human activity and the outcome of that activity (Giddens, 1979). Organizational structure helps define human activity, providing the rules and resources on which it is based; but structure is also created, reproduced, and potentially transformed by the same activity. As we saw in the previous chapter, the ways in which teachers like Tory and Bedford made sense of the standards were influenced by the very different opportunities that their school districts provided to support their sense-making. While organizational structure may not control district policymakers' and teachers' sense-making, it does influence it.

Notions of situation or place are more complex than I have treated them in this book. Hindsight is twenty-twenty; while the preceding chapters put people—district policymakers and teachers—and their organizational circumstances center stage in the implementation process, they fail to deal with the complexity of peoples' situation or place. Situation has to do with more than the particular school or school district in which a teacher or local policymaker works. Teachers' and district policymakers' situations in a career or life path are also likely important in understanding their sense-making. Recall Karen Bedford, the twenty-year veteran of Redwood public schools. Bedford's response to the standards was very much tied to where she was in her career and her boredom and disillusionment with teaching. These circumstances, coupled with shifts in the thrust of state and district policy, contributed to Bedford working to transform her mathematics teaching over a four-year period, making changes that, as she put it, "got me excited again." District policymakers' and teachers' situations are complex.

Policy Analysis

By the completion of this study, I had generated as many questions as I had answers. The cognitive perspective on implementation sketched in this book suggests an array of issues for future investigation. In particular, if we take the sense-making component of the implementation process seriously, then there are many unanswered concerns.

In the preceding chapters, I treated human sense-making chiefly in terms of cognitive scripts and prior knowledge. But sense-making also involves affect, and few studies have investigated the affective dimension of the implementation process (Hargreaves, 1998). Ann Smith's efforts to make sense of the science standards were in important ways tied to her drive to change science education for children. Reform ideas are frequently value-laden and connections between abstract ideas and deeply held values influence the sense-making process (Dunning, 1999;

Kunda, 1990). Emotional associations are part of knowledge structures and affect reasoning about value-laden issues (Ortony, Clore, and Collins, 1988). Moreover, changing existing behavior, the object of policy, affects one's self image. Relations between district policymakers' and teachers' values and emotions and their sense-making are not well understood. One potentially rich line of work then might explore the role of affect in district policymakers' and teachers' sense-making from and about policy.

Another line of work concerns the practice of sense-making. The preceding chapters offer only limited insights into the day-to-day practices that teachers and district policymakers engaged in as they figured out what standards meant and entailed for their work. District policymakers and teachers, like the rest of us, do not make sense of something in a single session; it takes time. We know relatively little about sense-making practice as it unfolds in curriculum committees, professional development meetings, grade-level meetings, classrooms, and informal interactions. Attempting to understand teachers' and district policymakers' sense-making from and about policy as a social practice would press scholars to move beyond an exclusive concern with implementing agents' knowledge structures and beliefs to explore the activity structures and relations that define their sense-making.

Policy Design

Policies that press radically new ideas require more complex cognitive shifts for district policymakers and teachers if they are to be understood; they demand that district policymakers and teachers change their existing knowledge scripts. Of course, some policies press more fundamental changes in existing behavior than others. Policies that encourage modest changes such as changing the sequencing of mathematics topics during the school year may be incorporated more easily into district policymakers' and teachers' existing scripts for teaching mathematics. The more fundamental the changes in existing behavior sought by a policy, the greater the extent to which existing scripts must be restructured in order to understand the new ideas—and in turn, the greater the implementation challenges. Transferring new ideas about instruction and its improvement from the capitol to the classroom is challenging, not because of the will of those in the district office or the schoolhouse, but because human sense-making tends to conserve existing understandings.

While human sense-making tends to be conserving, under certain conditions significant shifts in understanding are possible. The challenge for policymakers and reformers involves more than getting teachers to read and take seriously their policy proposals. A key part of the challenge involves designing policies that enable locals to understand the core reform ideas. State and federal policies cannot make sense for locals; they have to make their own sense of these ideas. Still, the design of policies influences locals' sense-making; some policies do better than others in enabling administrators and teachers to understand new ideas about classroom instruction. Much of the current conversation about policy design centers on policy instruments such as accountability mechanisms and inducements. Debates about the merits and demerits of different accountability mechanisms are plentiful and important. Yet picking the best combination of policy instruments is unlikely to be sufficient in helping local actors better understand policy.

If we take the sense-making aspect of the implementation process seriously, then the conversation needs to also focus on at least two other challenges. An especially influential dimension of policy design, rarely discussed in conventional accounts, concerns the *external representations* used by policymakers to convey their ideas for changing local practice. A cursory examination of policies suggests that the dominant approach to representing reform ideas is as a series of brief, one-sentence goals or objectives. Other external representations found less frequently in policy include extended essays that unpack the change ideas and attempt to justify them, as well as vignettes that illuminate the reform ideas in practice.

Part of the challenge here concerns managing the tension between the external representations—the new ideas—and local policymakers' and teachers' internal representations—their prior understanding. External representations that build on and engage locals' prior knowledge are more likely to help locals understand the reform ideas. Those who design policy may need to begin with district policymakers' and teachers' existing scripts in order to support local understanding. Policymakers might anticipate common misconceptions of core reform ideas and challenge these ideas. In addition, policymakers have to develop external representations that communicate the deeper underlying meaning rather than the surface features of the reform idea. The preceding chapters documented how district policymakers were likely to implement surface features of policy messages, missing deeper conceptual features. This happened because in making comparisons between existing understandings and new information, people have a tendency to focus on surface features. Psychologists tell us, however, that when individuals are told to draw comparisons that go beyond the surface features, they are likely to do so. Hence, policy representations that remind local actors to draw comparisons that go below the surface features are more likely to facilitate more substantive sense-making.

External representations exist fully only when individuals use them, and district policymakers and teachers used the standards in very different ways. The preceding chapters illuminate those circumstances that supported deeper understandings of the policy. First, classroom practice tended to be more of a public than a private, closed-door affair and deliberations about improving that practice were ongoing and central. Further, these deliberations focused not only on what the policy message meant, but also on teachers' efforts to put this message into practice. And finally, teachers and district policymakers used a variety of material resources, most notably classroom curricula, to support making sense of the reform ideas and of what these ideas entailed for their classroom practice.

Prospective

If my account is roughly right, the success of recent state and federal policy endeavors will depend in considerable measure on the local school district. State and federal agencies increasingly use student assessment and a variety of sanctions to hold schools accountable for student achievement. Recent federal legislation— No Child Left Behind, for example—requires (among other things) states to test students annually and holds schools accountable for tangible annual improvements in student achievement. Because education policymaking is not carried out in a federal- or state-controlled vacuum, district policymaking is likely to continue to expand in tandem with these state and federal initiatives. The fact that school districts are unlikely to take a back seat, coupled with state and federal agencies' limited infrastructure for influencing classroom instruction in far-flung classrooms, suggests that school-district policymaking will be critical to the success of these higher-level policies. Enlisting district policymakers is crucial.

The accountability mechanisms linked to student achievement and tied to tangible sanctions, a defining feature of recent federal and state education policy initiatives, are likely to get district policymakers' attention. The preceding chapters show how bigger sticks and juicier rewards can draw local attention to state and federal policies. But these instruments have limitations: absent opportunities to understand the core ideas about education pressed by these policies, district policymakers are likely to miss or misrepresent these ideas in local policies. If district policymakers fail to grasp the ideas about instruction pressed by policy, they cannot develop policies that support these ideas. As a result, the local effects of state and federal accountability mechanisms are likely to fall short of those intended by their designers absent attention to the opportunities that district policymakers and teachers have to make sense of policy messages.

Some commentators suggest that recent federal and state initiatives such as No Child Left Behind seek more modest changes in instruction, focusing more on students' mastery of basic skills. If this is the case, these initiatives may be less susceptible to being misunderstood by district policymakers and teachers. The more that policy ideas depart from district policymakers' and teachers' existing understandings and practices, the more likely they are to be misunderstood. While the implementation of all policies involves sense-making, policies that press more modest changes in existing practices are more likely to be constructed as intended by their designers. It is not obvious, however, that recent policy initiatives are centered exclusively on basic skills. For example, No Child Left Behind leaves it up to the states to define standards, proficiency levels, and assessments. Thus, the direction of the policy message will depend on the particular state. Of course, a critical question is whether states will retreat on the intellectual rigor of the content when many of their schools are identified as failing. Similarly, the federal requirement to test all grades may push states to move back to more standardized multiple-choice tests, which are cheaper to grade than tests that require written answers and explanations.

The cognitive perspective on implementation developed in this book supplements rather than supplants conventional accounts. It extends the explanatory power of conventional implementation models by taking into account district policymakers' and teachers' interpretations of the policy messages about mathematics and science education. The cognitive model allows for local policymakers' and teachers' rejection or revision of state policy to suit their own interests. For example, if district policymakers like

Sonny Naughton had constructed understandings that delved below the surface of the mathematics standards, they might have resisted such drastic changes to mathematics education. That is an empirical question beyond the scope of this book. Local resistance and capacity, which dominate conventional accounts, are also relevant considerations in a cognitive model of implementation.

Appendix

References

Index

Appendix: Research Methods

I used a multisite case study to gather and analyze data on the school district's role in the implementation of science and mathematics standards. This approach is well suited to in-depth analysis of complex processes (Miles and Huberman, 1984; Stake, 1995) such as policy implementation policy. The study involved three phases. Phase 1 investigated Michigan's state policy system for mathematics and science education. Phase 2 explored local governments' policy systems affecting mathematics and science education in nine Michigan school districts. Phase 3 explored the response of classroom teachers to the mathematics and science standards. The study involved mixed methods, including semi-structured interviews, surveys, observations, and document analysis.

A theoretical sampling strategy (Glaser and Strauss, 1967) was used to select nine school districts that varied as to geographical location, district size, social and ethnic composition of student population, and the district's reputation for innovation. Without some districts that were engaged in instructional reform, we would have been unable to get a sense of the approaches and activities that "active use districts" (Firestone, 1989) were pursuing, or a sense of what distinguished those districts from less responsive ones. To assess school districts' reputation for innovation, we spoke with knowledgeable observers, selecting five districts that were known for instructional innovation. The sample included three midsize city districts, two suburban districts, and four rural districts.

Data Collection

State-level data collected during Phase 1 of the study included interviews with state policymakers and observers of the system, state legislation, Department of Education (MDE) and state board policy documents, media reports, and state board minutes. Most of these data were collected between December 1992 and December 1993. The research team completed thirty-five interviews with state level informants. I also used interview and document data from an earlier study undertaken between 1989 and 1993. Further, we continued to collect state-level data until the completion of the study's third phase in 1996. Hence, our data collection at the state level covered a seven-year period from 1989 through 1996.

Phase 2 data, collected between September 1994 and August 1995, included interviews with school-district policymakers. District policy documents were also collected and analyzed. Beginning with the mathematics and science specialists in each district, a snowballing technique was used to identify for interview individuals involved in instructional policymaking. Those interviewed included district office and school administrators, teachers involved with making instructional policy, school board members, and parents. We completed 165 interviews.

Project researchers developed interview protocols, based on a review of the implementation literature and a consideration of instruments from other projects. Interview questions were open-ended and interviews ranged from forty-five minutes to two hours in duration; researchers worked to adapt questions to the particular informant and the information he or she was providing. Based on our analysis of interviews conducted during the first round, we developed a second interview protocol for a second round of data collection at the district level, which focused on four central issues.

Phase 3 of our study employed both quantitative and qualitative methods. We used the Population 1 (third- and fourth-grade) and Population 2 (seventh- and eighth-grade) Teacher Questionnaire of the Third International Mathematics and Science Study (TIMSS). In the fall of 1995, the TIMSS questionnaire was administered to all third- and fourth-grade teachers and all seventh- and eighth-grade mathematics and science teachers in the nine school districts. Of the 640 questionnaires distributed, 283 were returned, a response rate of 44 percent.

We then observed and interviewed a subsample of teachers based on their responses to the items on reform-oriented practice. Interviewing and observing teachers in the midst of recent reforms enabled researchers to map the progress of reform in practice, teasing out those dimensions of practice that teachers had changed and those dimensions they had left alone. We stratified the sample to ensure distribution across district types, geographical locations within the state, and teachers who scored high in mathematics, science, or both. Our subsample included teachers from six districts. We then selected randomly from among the teachers who reported teaching in a way that was more aligned with reformers' proposals, approximately the top 10 percent of our sample. We selected thirty-two teachers: eighteen third- or fourth-grade teachers, and seven seventh- or eighth-grade mathematics teachers. (The remaining seven teachers taught seventh- or eighth-grade science.) In the spring of 1996, we observed and interviewed each teacher twice, with one exception.

We used an observation protocol to take detailed notes and audiotaped parts of lessons. The mathematics observation protocol asked observers to attend to the content being taught as well as the teacher's pedagogy, including the task assigned to students, discourse patterns, and classroom environment. We wrote detailed narratives of the lesson we observed that addressed each of the analytical issues identified in the protocol. We also interviewed the teacher following each observation. Although we followed interview protocols, the questions were open-ended.

Data Analysis

The collection and analysis of data were integrated (Miles and Huberman, 1984) in all three phases. Analyzing interview, observation, and document data early in the study, we noticed issues that we pursued in subsequent interviews. This strategy enabled us to clarify working hypotheses that began to emerge from our initial analysis.

Phase 2 interview data were coded using a computer-based coding database developed specifically for the project. Our first round of interviews were coded using standard demographic data such as informant's role, district, gender, and eight coding categories: (1) interviewee's biography, (2) background information on the school district, (3) substantive ideas about mathematics and science education supported by district reform efforts, (4) nature and efficacy of district efforts to change mathematics and science education, (5) teachers' opportunities to learn about mathematics and science education in the school district, (6) local perspectives on state and federal policies and programs, (7) local responses to changes in state funding, and (8) influential factors on district initiatives concerning mathematics and science. We coded our second round of school-district interview data using four central categories. The first three concerned local educators' understanding of three themes—mathematics and science for "all students," "problem solving" in mathematics, and "hands-on" instruction in science. The fourth issue was parental involvement. Using these coded data, project researchers wrote case studies for each of the school districts and compared responses across informants and across districts for patterns of similarity and dissimilarity (Miles and Huberman, 1984).

We also undertook a more fine-grained analysis of different components of these coded data to explore some of the issues discussed in this book. To examine district policymakers' understandings of the mathematics and science standards, we recoded our interview data. With respect to mathematics, data coded under "substantive ideas about mathematics education supported by district reform efforts" were reanalyzed using eight coding categories taken from the mathematics standards and prominent themes identified from initial data analysis. The eight coding categories were problem solving, communication, cooperative learning, reasoning / understanding, active learning, hands-on manipulatives, real-world connections, and other subject integration. We also reanalyzed the data coded under "substantive ideas about mathematics education supported by district reform efforts" (round 1 interviews) and under district policymakers' understanding of "mathematics as problem solving" (round 2 interviews) using two central categories—form-focused understandings and function-focused understandings. Two subcategories—piecemeal understanding and demathematized understanding—were also used to identify and code patterns within form-focused understandings. These coding categories were developed from a close reading of a subsample (stratified by district and informants' role) of these coded data. Using these coding categories, we then recoded all data for the eighty-two interviewees in order to identify the salience of these patterns in district leaders' understanding of the mathematics reforms. We undertook a similar multistepped process for district policymakers' understanding of the science standards and an array of other issues. Where necessary we computed interrater reliability measures.

Phase 3 interview and observation data were systematically analyzed and integrated with the questionnaire data. Classroom observation and interview data were coded using categories that corresponded to the central themes in the mathematics and science standards as discussed in Chapter 2. Additional coding categories included "all students" and "influences" (concerning the array of factors that interact to shape teachers' attempts to revise their practice). The coding of data involved interpreting and organizing narrative accounts of the lessons and teachers' interview responses using the coding categories. These analyses resulted in analytical memos that ranged from forty to ninety single-spaced pages for each teacher. Researchers met as a group on a weekly basis for three-hour periods in the spring and throughout the summer to discuss write-ups of observation lessons and the coding of both observation and interview data. Teachers' coded data were subject to review by at least one other researcher before being considered complete. Due to personnel issues, for five teachers researchers worked primarily from completed narrative accounts of lessons and interview transcripts.

Using the survey data, we also identified a set of items related to the reforms that enabled us to construct a scale of standards-oriented practice for mathematics and science education. The mathematics standards-oriented instruction scale ranges from 0.5 to 9 with a mean of 6.67 and a standard deviation of 1.06. We determined the internal consistency of the scale using the Cronbach Alpha—a reliability measure that is acquired from calculating the average interitem correlation of the variables in the composite index. The measure ranges from 0 to 1 and the higher the correlation, the better the measure. The science standards-oriented instruction scale ranges from 1 to 4 with a mean of 2.31 and a standard deviation of 0.37. For the science scale, the reliability alpha is 0.76. Using the teacher's score on the standards-oriented scale as the dependent variable, we then constructed linear regression models to show teachers' sources of advice as a predictor of standards-oriented practice.

References

American Association for the Advancement of Science. (1989). *Science for all Americans.* Washington, D.C.

Anderson, C., and Smith, E. (1987). Teaching science. In V. Richardson-Koehler (Ed.), *Educators' handbook: A research perspective.* New York: Longman.

Bardach, E. (1982). Self-regulation and regulatory paperwork. In E. Bardach and R. Kagan (Eds.), *Social regulation: Strategies for reform.* San Francisco, Calif.: Institute for Contemporary Studies.

Becker, G. (1964). *Human capital.* New York: National Bureau of Economic Research.

Berman, P. (1978). The study of macro- and micro-implementation. *Public Policy, 26*(2).

Berman, P., and McLaughlin, M. (1977). *Federal programs supporting educational change. Vol. 7: Factors affecting implementation and continuation.* Santa Monica, Calif.: Rand Corporation.

Bourdieu, P. (1986). The forms of capital. In J. Richardson (Ed.), *Handbook of theory and research for the sociology of education.* New York: Greenwood Press.

Boyd, B. (1976). The public, the professionals, and educational policy making: Who governs? *Teachers College Record, 77*(4).

Brehm, J., and Gates, S. (1997). *Working, shirking, and sabotage: Bureaucratic response to a democratic public.* Ann Arbor: University of Michigan Press.

Brown, A. L., and Campione, J. C. (1990). Communities of learning and thinking, or a context by any other name. *Contributions to Human Development, 21.*

Brown, J., Collins, A., and Duguid, P. (1989). Situated cognition and the culture of learning. *Educational Researcher, 18.*

Butts, R., and Cremin, L. (1953). *A history of education in American culture.* New York: Holt.

Cantor, L. (1981). The growing role of states in American education. *Comparative Education, 16*(1).

Carey, S. (1985). *Conceptual change in childhood.* Cambridge, Mass.: MIT Press.

Chase, W., and Simon, H. (1974). Perception in chess. *Cognitive Psychology, 4.*

Chi, M., Feltovich, P., and Glaser, R. (1981). Categorization and representation of physics problems by experts and novices. *Cognitive Science, 5.*

Cohen, D. (1982). Policy and organization: The impact of state and federal educational policy on school governance. *Harvard Educational Review, 52*(1).

Cohen, D. (1996). Standards-based school reform: Policy, practice, and performance. In H. Ladd (Ed.), *Holding schools accountable.* Washington, D.C. : Brookings Institution.

Cohen, D., and Weiss, J. (1993). The interplay of social science and prior knowledge in public policy. In H. Redner (Ed.), *Studies in the thought of Charles E. Lindblom.* Boulder, Colo.: Westview.

Coleman, J. (1988). Social capital in the creation of human capital. *American Journal of Sociology, 94.*

Confrey, J. (1990). A review of the research on student conceptions in mathematics, science, and programming. In C. Cazden (Ed.), *Review of research in education,* vol. 16. Washington, D.C. : American Educational Research Association.

Cuban, L. (1993). *How teachers taught: Constancy and change in American classrooms, 1890–1990.* New York: Teachers College Press.

Dexter, E. (1922). *A history of education in the United States.* New York: Macmillan.

Doyle, W. (1983). Academic work. *Review of educational research, 53.*

Doyle W., and Carter, K. (1984). Academic tasks in classrooms. *Curriculum Inquiry, 14.*

Dunning, D. (1999). A newer look: Motivated social cognition and the schematic representation of social concepts. *Psychological Inquiry, 10*(1).

Educational evaluation and policy analysis (EEPA). (1990). Quarterly publication of the American Educational Research Association, *12*(3).

Elmore, R. F., and McLaughlin, M. W. (1988). *Steady work: Policy, practice and educational dissemination and change.* Santa Monica, Calif.: Rand Corporation.

Firestone, W. (1989). Using reform: Conceptualizing district initiative. *Educational Evaluation and Policy Analysis, 11*(2).

Firestone, W. A., Fitz, J., and Broadfoot, P. (1999). Power, learning, and legitimation: Assessment implementation across levels in the United States and the United Kingdom. *American Educational Research Journal, 36*(4).

Flavell, J. (1963). *The developmental psychology of Jean Piaget.* Princeton, N.J. : Van Nostrand.

Fuhrman, S. (1994). *Challenges in systemic reform.* New Brunswick, N.J. : Consortium for Policy Research in Education (CPRE), Rutgers University.

Fuhrman, S., and Elmore, R. (1990). Understanding local control in the wake of state education reform. *Educational Evaluation and Policy Analysis, 12*(1).

Fullan, M. (1991). *The new meaning of educational change.* New York: Teachers College Press.

Gentner, D. (1989). The mechanisms of analogical learning. In S. Vosniadou and A. Ortony (Eds.), *Similarity and analogical reasoning.* New York: Cambridge University Press.

Gentner, D., and Landers, R. (1985). Analogical reminding: A good match is hard to find. Paper presented at the International Conference on Systems, Man, and Cybernetics, Tucson, Ariz.

Gentner, D., Rattermann, M., and Forbus, K. (1994). The roles of similarity in transfer: Separating retrievability from inferential soundness. *Cognitive Psychology, 25.*

Giddens, A. (1979). *Central problems in social theory: Action, structure, and contradiction in social analysis.* Berkeley: University of California Press.

Glaser, B., and Strauss, A. (1967). *The discovery of grounded theory: Strategies for qualitative research.* Chicago: Aldine.

Goertz, M., Floden, R., and O'Day, J. (1995). *Studies of education reform: Systemic reform.* Consortium for Policy Research in Education (CPRE). New Brunswick, N.J. : Rutgers University.

Goodlad, J. (1984). *A place called school: Prospects for the future.* New York: McGraw-Hill.

Greeno, J. (1991). Number sense as situated knowing in a conceptual domain. *Journal for Research on Mathematics Education, 22.*

Hannaway, J., and Sproull, L. (1978–79). Who's running the show? Coordination and control in educational organizations. *Administrator's Notebook, 27.*

Hargreaves, A. (1998). The emotional practice of teaching. *Teaching and Teacher Education, 14*(8).

Hill, H. (1999). *Implementation networks: Nonstate resources for getting policy done.* Unpublished Ph.D. diss., University of Michigan, Ann Arbor.

Hill, H. (2001). Policy is not enough: Language and the interpretation of state standards. *American Educational Research Journal, 38*(2).

Hjern, B. (1982). Implementation research: The link gone missing. *Journal of Public Policy, 2.*

Kanter, R. (1983). *The change masters.* New York: Simon & Schuster.

Kirst, M., and Walker, D. (1971). An analysis of curriculum policymaking. *Review of Educational Research, 41.*

Kruglanski, A. (1980). Lay epistemologic process and contents: Another look at attribution theory. *Psychological Review, 87*(1).

Kunda, Z. (1990). The case for motivated reasoning. *Psychological Bulletin, 108.*

Lakatos, I. (1986). *Proofs and refutations.* Cambridge, Eng.: Cambridge University Press.

Lampert, M. (1990). When the problem is not the question and the solution is not the answer: Mathematical knowing and teaching. *American Educational Research Journal, 27*(1).

Lewis, D., and Maruna, S. (1998). Person-centered policy analysis. *Research in Public Policy Analysis and Management, 9.*

Lin, A. (2000). *Reform in the making: The implementation of social policy in prison.* Princeton, N.J. : Princeton University Press.

Lindblom, C. (1977). *Politics and markets.* New York: Basic Books.

Linder, S., and Peters, B. (1987). A design perspective on policy implementation: The fallacies of misplaced prescription. *Policy Studies Review,* 6(3).

Lipsky, M. (1980). *Street-level bureaucracy: Dilemmas of the individual in public services.* New York: Russell Sage Foundation.

Little, J. (1989). District policy choices and local professional development opportunities. *Educational Evaluation and Policy Analysis, 11*(2).

Lortie, D. (1975). *Schoolteacher: A sociological study.* Chicago: University of Chicago Press.

Mandler, J. (1984). *Stories, scripts, and scenes: Aspects of schema theory.* Hillsdale, N.J. : Lawrence Erlbaum.

Marris, P. (1975). *Loss and change.* New York: Anchor Press/Doubleday.

Mayer, D. (1999). Measuring Instructional Practice: Can Policymakers Trust Survey Data? *Educational Evaluation and Policy Analysis, 21*(1).

Mazmanian, D., and Sabatier, P. (1983). *Implementation and public policy.* Glenview, Ill.: Scott, Foresman, & Company.

McDonnell, L., and Elmore, R. (1987). Getting the job done: Alternative policy instruments. *Educational Evaluation and Policy Analysis, 9*(2).

McLaughlin, M. (1987). Learning from experience: Lessons from policy implementation. *Educational Evaluation and Policy Analysis, 9*(2).

McLaughlin, M. (1990). The Rand Change Agent Study revisited: Macro perspectives and micro realities. *Educational Researcher, 19*(9).

McLaughlin, M., and Shepard, L. (1995). *Improving education through standards-based reform.* Palo Alto, Calif.: Stanford University, National Academy of Education.

Meyer, J., and Rowan, B. (1978). The structure of educational organizations. In M. W. Meyer (Ed.), *Environments and organizations.* San Francisco: Jossey-Bass.

Meyer, J., and Scott, R. (with Rowan, B., and Deal, T.) (1983). *Organizational environments: Ritual and rationality.* Beverly Hills, Calif.: Sage.

Meyer, J., Scott, W., and Strang, D. (1987). Centralization, fragmentation, and school district complexity. *Administrative Science Quarterly, 32.*

Michigan State Board of Education. (1990). *Michigan essential goals and objectives for mathematics education.* Lansing, Mich.

Michigan State Board of Education. (1991). *Michigan essential goals and objectives for science education.* Lansing, Mich.

Michigan State Board of Education. (1992). *Model core curriculum outcomes.* Lansing, Mich.

Miles, M., and Huberman, M. (1984). *Qualitative data analysis: A source book of new methods.* Beverly Hills, Calif.: Sage.

Moessinger, P. (2000). *The paradox of social order: Linking psychology and sociology.* New York: Aldine de Gruyter.

National Council of Teachers of Mathematics (NCTM). (1989). *Curriculum and evaluation standards for school mathematics.* Reston, Va.

National Council of Teachers of Mathematics (NCTM). (1991). *Professional standards for teaching mathematics.* Reston, Va.

O'Day, J., and Smith, M. (1993). Systemic educational reform and educational opportunity. In Fuhrman, S. (Ed.), *Designing coherent educational policy.* San Francisco: Jossey-Bass.

Ortony, A., Clore, G., and Collins, A. (1988). *The cognitive structure of emotions.* New York: Cambridge University Press.

Peshkin, A. (1993). The goodness of qualitative research. *Educational Researcher, 22*(2).

Piaget, J. (1972). *The psychology of the child.* New York: Basic Books.

Porter, A. (1989). A curriculum out of balance: The case of elementary school mathematics. *Educational Researcher, 18*(5).

Portes, A. (1998). Social capital: Its origins and applications in modern sociology. *Annual Review of Sociology, 21*(1).

Ramirez, F., and Boli, J. (1987). The political construction of mass schooling: European origins and worldwide institutionalization. *Sociology of Education, 60*(1).

Resnick, L. (1988). Learning in school and out. *Educational Researcher, 16*(9).

Resnick, L. (1991). Shared cognition: Thinking as social practice. In L. Resnick, J. Levine, and S. Teasley (Eds.), *Perspectives on socially shared cognition.* Washington, D.C. : American Psychological Association (APA).

Romberg, T. (1983). A common curriculum for mathematics. In G. Fenstermacher and J. Goodlad (Eds.), *Individual differences and the common curriculum.* Chicago: National Society for the Study of Education.

Rowan, B. (1982). Organizational structure and the institutional environment: The case of public schools. *Administrative Science Quarterly, 27.*

Rumelhart, D. (1980). Schemata: The building blocks of cognition. In R. J. Spiro, B. Bruce, and W. F. Brewer (Eds.), *Theoretical issues in reading and comprehension.* Hillsdale, N.J. : Lawrence Erlbaum.

Sabatier, P. (1998). The advocacy coalition framework: Revisions and relevance for Europe. *Journal of European Public Policy, 5*(1).

Schank, R., and Abelson, R. (1977). *Scripts, plans, goals, and understanding.* Hillsdale, D.C. : Lawrence Erlbaum.

Schultz, T. (1961). Investment in human capital. *American Economic Review, 51.*

Smith, M., and O'Day, J. (1991). Systemic school reform. In S. Fuhrman and B. Malen (Eds.), *The politics of curriculum and testing.* New York: Falmer Press.

Spillane, J. (1996). School districts matter: Local educational authorities and state instructional policy. *Educational Policy, 10*(1).

Stake, R. E. (1995). *The art of case study research.* Thousand Oaks, Calif.: Sage.

Stake, R., and Easley, J. (1978). *Case studies in science education* (No. 038–000–00377–1). Washington, D.C.: Government Printing Office.

Starbuck, W., and Milliken, F. (1988). Executives' perceptual filters: What they notice and how they make sense. In D. Hambrick (Ed.), *The executive effect: Concepts and methods for studying top managers.* Greenwich, Conn.: JAI.

Stein, M., Grover, B., and Henningsen, M. (1996). Building student capacity for mathematical thinking and reasoning: An analysis of mathematical tasks used in reform classrooms. *American Educational Research Journal, 33*(2).

Stone, D. (1988). *Policy paradox and political reason.* Boston: Little, Brown.

Strike, K., and Posner, G. (1985). A conceptual change view of learning and understanding. In L. H. T. West and A. L. Pines (Eds.), *Cognitive structure and conceptual change.* Orlando, Fla.: Academic Press.

Thompson, C., Spillane, J., and Cohen, D. K. (1994). *The state policy system affecting science and mathematics education in Michigan.* Lansing: Michigan Statewide Systemic Initiative Policy and Program Review Component.

Tyack, D., and Hansot, E. (1982). *Managers of virtue: Public school leadership in America, 1820–1980.* New York: Basic Books.

Tyack, D., and Tobin, W. (1994). The grammar of schooling: Why has it been so hard to change? *American Educational Research Journal, 31*(3).

Van Meter, D., and Van Horn, C. (1975). The policy implementation process: A conceptual framework. *Administration and Society, 6*(4).

von Glasersfeld, E. (1989). Cognition, construction of knowledge, and teaching. *Synthese, 80*(1).

Weick, K. (1995). *Sensemaking in organizations.* Thousand Oaks, Calif.: Sage.

Weiss, J. (1990). Ideas and inducements in mental health. *Journal of Policy Analysis and Management, 19*(2).

Wilson, J. (1989). *Bureaucracy: What government agencies do and why they do it.* New York: Basic.

Winters, S. (1990). Integrating Implementation Research. In D. Palumbo and D. Calista (Eds.), *Implementation and the Policy Process.* New York: Greenwood Press.

Wirt, R., and Kirst, M. (1997). *The political dynamics of American education.* Berkeley, Calif.: McCutchan Press.

Wise, A. (1979). *Legislated learning.* Berkeley: University of California Press.

Wolf, S., Borko, H., Elliott, R., and McIver, M. (2000). "That dog won't hunt!" Exemplary school change efforts within the Kentucky reform. *American Educational Research Journal, 37*(2).

Yanow, D. (1996). *How does a policy mean?* Washington, D.C.: Georgetown University Press.

Index

James P. Spillane is Associate Professor of Education and Social Policy, Northwestern University.